Quit Your Job and Grow Some Hair

Quit Your Job and Grow Some Hair

Gary N. Rubin, Ph.D.

Impact Publications
Manassas Park, VA

Library of Congress Cataloging-in-Publication-Data

Library of Congress Cataloguing-in-Publication Data

Gary N. Rubin
    Quit your job and grow some hair: know when to go, when to stay / Gary N. Rubin
        p. cm.
    Includes index.
    ISBN 1-57023-191-5   2002112578

Publisher: For information on Impact Publications, including current and forthcoming publications, authors, press kits, online bookstore, and submission requirements, visit our website: www.impactpublications.com.

Publicity/Rights: For information on publicity, author interviews, and subsidiary rights, contact the Media Relations Department: Tel. 703-361-7300, Fax 703-335-9486, or email: info@impactpublications.com.

Sales/Distribution: All bookstore sales are handled through Impact's trade distributor: National Book Network, 15200 NBN Way, Blue Ridge Summit, PA 17214, Tel. 1-800-462-6420. All other sales and distribution inquiries should be directed to the publisher: Sales Department, IMPACT PUBLICATIONS, 9104 Manassas Drive, Suite N, Manassas Park, VA 20111-5211, Tel. 703-361-7300, Fax 703-335-9486, or email: info@impactpublications.com.

Contents

Acknowledgments

Special thanks to Ron and Caryl Krannich at Impact Publications for their guidance in providing recommended resources for this book. Your support has been invaluable.

Special thanks to my friends Lawrence and Ellen Land for their support and confidence in me throughout this project.

I dedicate this book to my wife, Nancy, and my daughter, Elizabeth, whose constant encouragement and unwavering support gave me the strength and resolve to move forward.

Quit Your Job and Grow Some Hair

1

An Exciting Journey
Into the Unknown

There **is no question** the world has changed since September 11. It has changed in ways we would not have imagined possible. These changes have helped put our own personal world in perspective. In some ways we have become more focused on things much larger than ourselves—our families, our country, world peace, the planet. The ordinary things we used to worry about—our jobs, our physical appearance, our material possessions, or where we should take a vacation—now seem unimportant, mundane, and shallow. We have become more concerned with our physical security than our financial and job security.

Yet in the wake of the horrific events of September 11, many have found themselves out of jobs and dealing with the personal anxiety of that reality coupled with anxiety about our world. Even individuals in top-management or high-profile positions find themselves, with downsizing and consolidation, the stock market plunge, and the Enron fallout, worried about their careers and their futures. In fact, if they are truly "reading the tea leaves," they know they need to go, and this realization will call for plans and strategies for leaving and beginning anew.

For others the events of September 11 and its aftermath, while superimposing a pall on life in general, have not changed the everyday reality that they are deeply unhappy in their jobs and find their lives less and less fulfilling. For them, the alternatives are whether or not they should quit their jobs because of this unhappiness or keep them because job insecurity might even be more painful. Yet they are also being influenced by September 11th's most important lesson of all: the uncertainty of life. If that is true, shouldn't they spend their days doing something that is personally meaningful?

It is this author's view that the answer to this question is a resounding YES and the only solution to this conundrum is to move forward.

As we live longer, the chances of us making three or four significant career changes in our lifetime will become less and less of an anomaly. While some of us are very comfortable and secure in our jobs or careers, others are burned out in their professions, stressed out from all the pressures, spending less time with friends or loved ones, or doing tasks that are personally unfulfilling. More importantly, from a professional point of view, their creative juices may be drying up and their ability to look at things from new perspectives is diminishing. As I reflect on my own career changes, these are some of the factors that influenced me to change, and perhaps they mirror your own. Regardless of what motivates you, knowing when to go or knowing when to stay involves a multi-layered decision-making process that is both emotional and pragmatic.

Fifteen years ago, I was a tenured professor and administrator at a major statewide university. I was widely respected by my peers and was moving up the ladder in the university system. In addition to my university responsibilities, I had a human relations consulting business on the side, was heavily involved in numerous volunteer activities, and was considered a leader in the community. My wife was very often a partner in these activities and, as a result, we enjoyed the benefits of being perceived as one of the up and coming young couples in the area. Yet, something was missing. I was growing tired of university politics and was spending more and more time in my community activities. The idea of changing careers or making my avocation my profession was intensifying. Ultimately, I made the decision to do just that. At 37, sacrificing academic tenure and financial security, I moved into another profession at a lesser salary, a demoted title, and to the dismay of my friends and colleagues who thought I had absolutely "lost it." "Why would you do this?" was their constant refrain.

Yet, all along my inner voice told me this was the right thing to do, and that was the voice I listened to. With the help of an extremely supportive spouse, I did it and it worked!

In retrospect, it was a great deal simpler then. I was in my thirties. I had no serious financial constraints even though we had just had our daughter, Elizabeth. While changing from my core profession to something totally different and without any guarantees was risky, it was also exciting. I was entering a profession where I had a mission, a calling if you will, that could not go unanswered. So, after more than a dozen years in higher education, I moved into nonprofit management in an agency dedicated to raising money to support social service needs. It was, indeed, an uncharted course but a course I was compelled to take.

Incidentally, in that same year after being married more than 14 years and becoming new parents, we moved to a new home and bought two new cars. This could have been an extremely stressful time since, on the continuum of life stresses, changing careers, having children, and making major financial commitments are at the top. But for us, it was our most joyous time because it was our **choice**. We had **control**. We orchestrated the changes. Change can be wonderful as long as **you** control it.

The same philosophy was applicable when I made my second major career change seven years later, when I decided to pick up stakes after living 21 years in one place to move to Florida. All of this for an opportunity that was not at all secure but could bring greater financial benefit, a chance for new challenges, professional growth, and an opportunity to be with family, something we had never had before. While this change was certainly not as potentially stressful as the first, the idea of relocating brought new anxieties. Fortunately, these were at a minimum.

Fast-forward more than eight years. The kind of change I am chronicling here is very different. To be truthful, this change has been much scarier. Age, finances, and having the responsibility of a child who will soon be in college can make a great deal of difference in your psyche as you begin your process of change. Yet, at the same time, it can be exciting once you make that decision, develop a plan, and methodically follow a course of action. I won't tell you now the final outcome of my journey, now for I want you to be involved until the end of this book, but I will say that these three points of change have been the most invigorating and renewing times of my life. In fact my wife insists that since I began my latest journey, I, who have been follically challenged for many years, have not only grown person-ally and professionally but also have grown more hair as the weeks and months go by.

This book is not the product of scientific inquiry but, instead, is based on 30 years of experience working, stopping work, and beginning anew. It is also reflective of the experiences of friends, former colleagues, and others who have traveled similar paths in their efforts to find personal and professional satisfaction.

This is a book about me. It's a book about you. It's about any-one who has been in a situation they want to get out of but don't know how. It's a book about freedom and liberation on a very per-sonal level. It's about separating, the anxiety that goes along with it, and the steps that can carry you through it. In this case, it's about my separation from a top management position, but the principles outlined here could apply to any major life change because, in essence, this is a book about **letting go**.

For me, maybe it was turning 50. Maybe it was just a feeling that I was tired of being in a career where I had to worry about what my cohorts were thinking. Maybe, more than anything else, it was a feeling of not being in control. Maybe it was read-ing the tea leaves and knowing what was coming down the pike. Maybe it was all those things that ultimately caused me to decide to move forward. Regardless of the reasons, I could only fool myself for so long.

Let this book be a blueprint, a survivor's guide, if you will, for helping you reach separation, if indeed that's the right course, and in the process, getting yourself together, perhaps more than ever before.

2

Signs of the Times

*"Again, it's Monday. How many more Mondays will
I have to dread getting dressed and going to work?"*

What are the signs? What are those signs that are telling you that you need to change direction professionally? Do you wake up every morning with a lump of dread in your throat? Do you lie in bed a little longer hoping it will dissipate? Does a second wave of depression come over you as you are brushing your teeth? Do you start taking St. John's Wort and kava to make you feel you can control your feelings? Do you need that first cup of morning coffee—that jolt of caffeine—to pick you up psychologically as well as physically, knowing that it will only buy you a half-hour of false reality before true reality sets in? Do you get to the office after your "Starbuck's Break," dreading the rest of the day, looking at your calendar and literally counting the hours until it's over?

Is it avoiding real interaction with people only to find safety and comfort when using your cell phone? Is it calling your wife for no good reason (not even to have a conversation), but only to know she is there? Is it getting emotional when you are by yourself because you feel hopeless and not worthy?

If these are the feelings and emotions you are experiencing, you know you are in pain. You're angry. You may even be close to depression, and the pain and the anger have got to stop. As the character Howard Beale, played by Peter Finch, in the film *Network* says, "You're mad as hell and you're not going to take it anymore!"

Telling Signs of Change

While the feelings I just described project an overall state of mind, the following signs relate more specifically to your professional well being. Check those that apply to you.

☐ Have You Lost the Passion and Excitement for What You're Doing?

Have the drive and commitment you once had for your work and the mission of your organization been put on automatic pilot? Do you find yourself just going through the motions, doing the same thing, recycling old ideas, and settling for less? If this is the case, you're certainly not bringing added value to your work and, in the process, only diminishing your feelings of self-worth and productivity. Whereas once accomplishing the work and producing results were a challenge, has it now turned to fear and loathing of having to get it done? If this is where you're at, isn't it time to make a change?

☐ Are You Questioning What You Know You Do Well?

Do you have self-doubts about your professional competence and effectiveness? All of us in our professional and personal lives begin to sort out and identify not only what we do well but what we do better than most of our peers. We begin to understand the **power** we possess in certain circumstances due to a particular talent, skill, or instinct we've acquired and developed. For some, it might be public speaking, for others it might be business savvy, and for others it might be the ability to make judgments about human relations. Even with all of our other insecurities, this special power gives us confidence and strength. And we need it. We need to know that we have at least one thing, one talent that when, using it, we **rule**.

When that power, the feeling we have about it, or our reluctance to access it begins to wane, or in the worse circumstances seems to be lost, something is wrong. When Samantha's twitch could no longer get the desired results, or Clark Kent's Superman could no longer muster up the strength and the will, the root of their incapacity to do what they knew they could do was often stymied by their surrounding circumstances. Like them, you may be involuntarily inhibited from utilizing the power you know you have. It's not that the opportunities aren't there. You just don't feel able to exercise it.

☐ Are You Feeling Like You Don't Know Where to Begin?

Two things I've always prided myself on are my organizational skills and my ability to set priorities for a particular day. While many of us have become compulsive list makers, I actually made them and used them. However, prior to making my own personal decision to leave, coming to the office every day was colored by a feeling of being totally overwhelmed, not knowing where to begin, not being able to make my list, let alone acting on it.

Despair and chaos were the rule. What in the environment or within me was making me feel this way? It becomes a Catch 22. The more you feel overwhelmed, the less you are able to act, and the more overwhelmed you feel. If this describes your situation, what conditions or elements in your present environment are causing you to feel this way? Part of the answer may come from within you, but part of it may be from your surroundings.

☐ Are You Keeping Things Closed and Close to the Vest?

If you've read Signs #1, 2, and 3, you might conclude that one of the remedies would be to get help from your colleagues and others outside your situation. However, the combination of #1, 2, and 3 make this impossible!

The more you feel a loss of power, the more you feel overwhelmed and the more unlikely you are (until it becomes unbearable) to seek help. In fact, you begin to keep things more to yourself, communicating less with others. You begin to trust less and let paranoia take over. You lack the security to let anyone know what you don't know. You become more insular. You begin to feel more competitive and defensive with your colleagues. You escape to your car to avoid interaction, or you find yourself closing the door to your office more often. While all of us experience isolated instances like this, when it becomes a pattern of behavior that is beginning to define your personality, the more you need to face the fact that this sign is becoming a permanent pothole in the road.

❒ Are You Focusing on the Small Stuff?

When you're at the point when the smallest tasks, the most mundane, are overwhelming you or you're spending all of your time focusing on insignificant matters, then something is wrong. You're trying to fill your time by ignoring the larger issues you need to face. You're losing your grip and becoming flooded by self-doubt. You may even be in a constant state of panic, a feeling that you cannot do anything right. Isn't it time to assess what is going on in your life?

☐ Is Your Appearance Mirroring Your Negative Feelings?

Have you analyzed what you have been wearing lately? Are you choosing darker colors? Is wearing the new jacket or outfit you bought over the weekend (when you were detached from the everyday reality and you rewarded yourself with new attire) not bringing you any joy on Monday? Are you wearing clothes or acting in ways to make yourself appear invisible? It has nothing to do with being conservative or businesslike. Instead, you're losing a sense of who you are. You want to disappear.

In addition to your attire, have you noticed how you've looked lately? I once had a professor who said, "If you don't get your strokes, your spine shrivels up." What an apt description. All of us have seen individuals who seem to be pulled down by the weight of the world or the weight of their job. They're stooped over, their shoulders are hunched, their mouths sagging. Have you looked in the mirror lately? Is this beginning to sound and look like you?

☐ Are You Only Living in the Here and Now?

Some philosophers would suggest that we should live in the "here and now." We should savor every moment and not get caught up in the trivia that is going on around us. It's hard to argue with this philosophy. It becomes something else, however, when we're only living in the "here and now" because we have lost our ability to dream and think in the long term because we're so desperately caught up in trying to survive the moment. When the motivation to live in the "here and now" is not the continuous search for self-actualization but, rather, a loss of desire to look toward the future, isn't this a time for change?

❏ Is It Becoming Harder and Harder to Conceal Your Inner Feelings and Your Stress?

While all of us hide or shield our true feelings from others to some degree or put a spin on what's happening in our lives, this is different than trying to mask a pervasive attitude characterized by fear and stress that seems to permeate all aspects of our lives. This becomes even more difficult and with more consequences if we are public figures or high-profile CEOs and are expected to be the cheerleaders for our organization. We can only hide our overall state of mind for so long before the veneer begins to crack. We let our hair down at off moments. Haven't each of us watched others when they didn't know we were watching? It's like witnessing an actor or actress getting ready to go onstage before getting into character. Haven't we seen a photograph of ourselves when we didn't know it was being taken? Are we really fooling anyone, let alone ourselves?

☐ Are You Lashing Out at Those Who Mean the Most to You?

A colleague of mine who had just made the decision to leave his job told me, "I don't know how many times during the two years prior to my decision to separate from my job my wife said to me, 'Can't you treat me like you treat people in your job?'" What she meant was that during the day he was bending over backwards to accommodate and please everyone, hiding any anger and resentment, while at home spending the precious hours they had together venting his frustrations.

All of us experience days when everything seems to be going wrong and in many instances it has absolutely nothing to do with our jobs or the work setting. Yet often that is the reason. When we find ourselves spending our off hours obsessing over what went wrong at work, isn't it time to figure out why this is so before we allow the situation to erode our most important relationships?

☐ Are You Only Focusing on Your Inadequacies?

Do you walk into your office only thinking about what you can't do rather than what you can do? If every decision and action is prefaced with hesitation and self-doubt coupled with feelings of inadequacy and failure, this state of mind can only lead to more despair and a continuous game of career survival rather than career renewal. If all your years of success and accomplishment seemed to be canceled out by your inability to feel empowered to get the job done, not being able to get it done will become a self-fulfilling prophecy. Isn't it time to feel good about yourself again?

☐ Are You Losing All Balance in Your Life?

Have your stress and concern about your professional well-being taken over your life? Do you find that it's all you can talk about or think about on or off the job? Do you find yourself having more and more difficulty engaging in conversation with your spouse, your children, and your friends? Has your sense of fun and joy in going to a movie, watching a football game, or having dinner with friends at a restaurant diminished to the point where you don't even want to go? There is no question that if this is your state of mind, your life is out of balance and you better try to get it back before it weighs you down so much that your physical and mental health are totally compromised.

It is unlikely that you are experiencing all of these signs at the same time, or that they are as distinct as they are characterized here. However, you may be experiencing each of these with varying intensity as well as others that are all saying to you, "You need to make a change!"

Ask Yourself

We may try to fool those around us but we cannot fool ourselves. We already know or have known for a long time how our job and career are affecting us. However, our powers of denial can be very influential in not allowing us to truly address those feelings. The following exercise, while totally subjective, can be helpful in having you raise the appropriate questions and take appropriate action.

Activity A

For a two-week period keep a diary of your feelings toward your work environment, focusing on the following dimensions:

1. Professional satisfaction

2. Feelings of job insecurity and inadequacy

3. Feelings of being overwhelmed

4. Feelings of aloneness

5. Overall stress

6. Decrease in your effectiveness

7. Personal satisfaction

Activity B

Once you have kept the diary, analyze and summarize it by asking the following questions:

1. What is the overall professional and personal satisfaction profile your diary entries suggest?

2. Are these feelings a product of a particular moment in time, the stress of a particular project or deadline, or a temporary personnel or personality issue with a colleague, supervisor, or client? Or do they reflect an ongoing issue?

3. What is your work environment doing to your productivity, creativity, sense of empowerment, and self-image?

4. How would you evaluate your physical and mental well-being? What impact is your job having on these two dimensions?

5. Have you had these feelings before? Are the feelings a by-product of the job or your response to it?

Recommended Resources

Books

Career Change, David P. Helfand (McGraw-Hill, 1999)

Change Your Job, Change Your Life, Ron Krannich (Impact Publications, 2002)

Dare to Change Your Life, Carole Kanchier (JIST Publishing, 2000)

Do What You Are, Paul D. Tieger and Barbara Barron-Tieger (Little Brown & Company, 2001)

Discover What You're Best At, Linda Gale (Fireside, 1998)

Do What You Love for the Rest of Your Life: A Practical Guide to Career Change and Personal Renewal, Bob Griffiths (Ballantine Books, 2001)

I Could Do Anything If Only I Knew What It Was: How to Discover What You Really Want and How to Get It, Barbara Sher (Dell Publishing Company, 1995)

Is It Too Late to Run Away and Join the Circus?, Marti Diane Smye (John Wiley & Sons, 2001)

It's Only Too Late If You Don't Start Now: How to Create Your Second Life at Any Age, Barbara Sher (Dell Publishing Company, 1999)

Making a Living Without a Job: Winning Ways for Creating Work That You Live, Barbara J. Winter (Bantam Doubleday Dell, 1993)

The Pathfinder: How to Choose or Change Your Career for a Lifetime of Satisfaction and Success, Nicholas Lore (Fireside, 1998)

Rites of Passage at $100,000 to $1 Million+: Your Insider's Lifetime Guide to Executive Job-Changing and Faster Career Progress in the 21st Century, John Lucht (Henry Holt & Company, 2000)

Starting Over: How to Change Careers or Start Your Own Business, Stephen M. Pollan and Mark Levin (Warner Books, 1997)

What Color Is Your Parachute?, Richard Nelson Bolles (Ten Speed Press, 2002)

Who Moved My Cheese? An Amazing Way to Deal With Change in Your Work and in Your Life, Spencer Johnson (Putnam Publishing Group, 1998)

Websites

- CareerHub   careerhub.com
                                      cpp-db.com

- CareerLab.com   careerlab.com

- Self-Directed Search®   self-directed-search.com

- Personality Online   spods.net/personality

- Keirsey Character Sorter   keirsey.com

- MAPP™   assessment.com

- PersonalityType   personalitytype.com

- Analyze My Career   analyzemycareer.com

- Birkman Method   review.com/career/article.cfm?id=
                                 career/car_quiz_intro

- Career Key   ncsu.edu/careerkey

- CareerLeader™ www.careerdiscovery.com/careerleader

- Career Services Group   careerperfect.com

- Careers By Design®   careers-by-design.com

- College Board   myroad.com

- Emode   www.emode.com/emode/careertest.jsp

- Enneagram   ennea.com

- Fortune.com   fortune.com/careers

- Futurestep   futurestep.com

- Humanmetrics   humanmetrics.com

- Interest Finder Quiz   myfuture.com/
                                      career/interest.html

- Jackson Vocational Interest Inventory   jvis.com

- Keirsey Character Sorter   keirsey.com

- OnlineProfiles   onlineprofiles.com

- People Management   www.jobfit-pmi.com
  International

- Personality and IQ Tests   www.davideck.com

- Profiler   profiler.com

- QueenDom   queendom.com

- Tests on the Web   2h.com

3

Knowing When to Stay

"Did I over-react? Could I have stayed longer?"

While this book focuses on those signs which suggest you need to totally separate from your professional situation, and the steps that can help you in that decision, many of us don't need to go to such an extreme. Instead we may need to find ways to rejuvenate and renew ourselves in our current job or career. To achieve this, we need to make an honest assessment of what works and what doesn't. Can the negative factors be eliminated or minimized, or have we reached an untenable situation that can't be rectified?

Very often, when one thing is terribly wrong, it cancels out all that is positive. We allow that one factor to take on too much importance. Whatever the reasons, in conducting your assessment the following elements need to be considered:

Your Emotional Well Being

We all know that the way we feel about ourselves affects everything we do, both personally and professionally. If you answered yes to all or a majority of the signs in Chapter 2 and concluded that it is the job that is making you unhappy, then you have no choice but to leave, because you are in a debilitating situation and one that will only get worse. All the job security in the world and all the prestige and status that your position provides cannot be exchanged for your mental or physical health. Yes, there are trade-offs in any career, however, these are ones you can ill afford to make.

The Professional Match

☐ Is this position what you thought it was going to be?

☐ Are you doing the kind of work you anticipated?

☐ Do you have a clear job description?

☐ Are the expectations for job performance defined?

☐ Are the awards for doing a good job understood by you and your superior?

☐ Do you understand the evaluation process?

If the professional match is not a perfect fit (there is no such thing) where is it on your continuum of job satisfaction? Is it a position that can be re-crafted to ultimately meet your professional needs? If not, your frustration will increase and your performance level will eventually diminish. You could find yourself caught in a position you didn't want in the first place, but with an exit initiated by your employer and not by you.

How Stuck Are You?

There is probably nothing worse than being in a situation where you feel stuck and you see no way out. Have you analyzed why you feel stuck? Very often, the degree of "stuckness" may be due to your financial situation. You feel you can't afford to leave. A meeting with your accountant or a financial planner can give you a clear assessment of your financial security and whether or not it is truly a reason for staying. However, many of us use "finances" as a justification for not changing when in fact our real reason for staying is related to the negative feelings we have about ourselves, our abilities and our talents and our fear of never again being gainfully employed if we leave our current position.

Very often it is the job itself that is making us feel this way. Are you in a job that depletes or doesn't use your creative talents and creative instincts? Is the repetitive nature of your current situation resulting in unbearable boredom and complacency? Worse, is it making you feel unworthy or less valuable to your organization? If you've answered yes, what are your chances of getting unstuck?

What Are Your Options?

The ultimate question that needs to be answered is what are your options? One option, of course, is to make the decision to leave, the primary focus of this book. But, the other option is to see what can be done in your present environment to provide what you need both professionally and personally. Here are some suggestions:

1. Re-define Your Job Description

Do you even have a job description? You may not, and much of your frustration, stress, and insecurity about your job may be related to a lack of clarity. What are the expectations for your position and the criteria for evaluating your performance? Are there opportunities for growth and development? Getting clarity may begin with crafting your own job description. Likewise, if there is a formal job description, can it be retuned and refined? Again, be proactive and craft your own vision of your job description.

To help you with this, you might contact professional colleagues within your industry or business and compare job descriptions. Going on the Internet and reading job openings for your type of position to glean areas of responsibility can also be useful. Frame of reference is very important in knowing if your expectations and sense of reality are in sync with the marketplace.

2. Check Out the Possibilities Within Your Organization

Are you in an organization that promotes and rewards people from within? If it does, what is the usual timetable for this to occur and what are the steps you need to take?

It could be that you need to acquire additional skills or proficiencies in particular areas. For instance if your position is calling for more and more opportunities for you to represent the organization in the community, perhaps you need to become more skilled in public speaking. Is there a Toastmasters chapter within your organization or community? Is a public speaking module being offered at a national meeting you will be attending? Looking for opportunities to enhance your computer skills, fiscal management skills, or even guidance on dress and corporate etiquette could make the difference in leading you to other positions within the organization, as well as rejuvenating yourself and your feelings about the job. Anything you can do to provide added value to the organization will make you that much more indispensable and at the same time increase your feelings of self-worth.

If cost is a factor in getting additional training, perhaps the organization will pay for you to attend professional development workshops, take college classes, or even provide tuition assistance for a degree program. Even if they don't, the fact that you are inquiring demonstrates your personal initiative and desire to move ahead.

If you are already in the top position, can the focus of your responsibilities change to provide you greater flexibility, creativity, and less of a chance of burnout?

For instance, if you are the top sales manager within the organization but you no longer feel challenged or excited about your work, would a change in your "territory" make a difference in your attitude? Would taking on an associate or developing a mentor/mentee relationship with someone new to the organization give you personal fulfillment and remind you of the depth, experience, and value you bring to the organization?

Finally, sometimes a lateral move in the organization can be the answer. Review job postings on your company's website for current openings. You might find a list of positions you were totally unaware of, and no one will know you were even looking—thus enabling you to have anonymity in your career quest. For many, moving to a higher position within the corporate hierarchy might not be a desirable strategy. Instead, they might seek to work with other colleagues or to work in a new division or on a new project. The financial rewards might stay the same but the psychological and emotional awards could be great. While moving up can sometimes lead to the "Peter Principle" (reaching your level of incompetence), moving across can lead to personal harmony and satisfaction.

3. Assess Your Collegial Relationships

Decisions to leave are often made because of personality conflicts within the organization.

Sometimes, they are made prematurely. The first thing you need to ask yourself is whether or not this relationship can change. What is the root of the conflict? Is it issue-based or personality-based? If it's the former, perhaps you can deal with this through a supervisor, human resources director, or an intermediary within the organization. In many instances, talking out an issue with a neutral party, who facilitates discussion and keeps it focused on issues, can clear up misunderstandings or highlight information that will make a difference in the relationship between two fellow employees.

If the issue is personality-based and the professional demands require working together, there may not be an easy solution. Sometimes the only alternatives are to change the reporting structure or make a move to another division within the organization.

In assessing your relationships with your colleagues to determine whether you should leave or stay, you need to consider their (1) longevity in the organization, (2) your contact with them, and (3) their professional capital within the organization. Are you giving these relationships too much importance? Do you have too high an opinion of your perceived adversary? Your decision to go, for the most part, should not be based on another person, even if that individual is the decision-maker or your current supervisor. Before you pick up your marbles, check to see how long he'll be in the game. That person may be out of there before you know it, and your perception of the organizational climate could be turned around completely.

This is particularly true in an environment where mergers, acquisitions, downsizing, and buy-outs have become fairly routine, not only within large corporations but medium-size organizations as well. Changes in top management, whether at the CEO or vice-presidential level, are commonplace and the opportunities for career advancement for individuals situated at lower rungs of the corporate ladder may be possible. Does the following story sound familiar?

The Vice-President of the marketing division of a major corporation had been the fair-haired child of the CEO for over five years. While the Associate V.P. was doing all the creative work and coming up with the vision for practically every campaign, the V.P. was taking all the credit because he had the ear of the CEO and was a great salesman. No execution but a great salesman. All smoke and mirrors, but thanks to the creative talents of the Associate V.P., he would always come out on top. No one seemed to recognize this. However, the pressure, the hidden resentment and anger of the Associate V.P., and the abuse he had taken from his boss had become so intolerable he had begun the process of leaving the organization for a much lesser paying job. Two weeks before he was to leave, the firm changed hands and a new CEO took over. The reality of how the V.P. had maintained success came out, and the Associate V.P. was designated the new V.P. for Marketing.

While talk of consolidation or buy-out of this firm had been in the air for a long time, the Associate V.P. had not paid attention to the chatter in his environment and, as a result, nearly lost an opportunity.

The lesson to be learned from this example is that as a top professional in a competitive and changing industry you must be attuned to your workplace and assess how that environment might be changing. While too much of this analysis can lead to paranoia and excessive gamesmanship, it can also lead to your professional advancement.

4. Talk to People

Very often our pride and our ego do not allow us to seek counsel. This is particularly true as we move up the ladder in a company or organization. It must be first understood that everyone—and I mean everyone at various times in their lives—needs support and perspective from other people. Even the Pope needs divine guidance. It is not a sign of weakness and in many instances can be a sign of great strength.

The fundamental question becomes whom do I ask? More than that, whom do I trust? Talking to colleagues **within your organization** for information, clarification, or ideas is fine, but discussing personal problems, conflicts with fellow employees, or questions related to staying or leaving the organization should be avoided. The typical organizational grapevine has strong roots and you want to be sure your concerns don't provide fertile ground for the rumor mill.

Talking to people who have similar positions to your own or work **outside your organization**, but in a similar environment, can give you a much better perspective on your situation. Ask them these questions:

❏ Is their job fulfilling to them?

❏ Is their job description similar to yours, or are there major differences?

❏ Are there elements or features of their job that can be integrated into your own?

You may find that you're not taking advantage of opportunities at your own organization. Maybe you don't have to leave but just need to maximize or modify what you're presently doing.

Even if you're the CEO, you need to talk to **someone**. Don't go it alone.

5. Be a Change Agent

Is the mission of the organization something that you totally embrace, or is it the root cause of your unhappiness? If the latter, this is fundamental for, while you may change, chances are the mission will not and may be reason enough for you to leave. On the other hand, can **you** be a change agent for the organization? While this may be easier to accomplish in a small organization or business, you can very often be the catalyst for change within a division or department. If you can, this may be the reason to stay, for having an impact on the organization will not only help to move it to the next level but will be personally and professionally fulfilling.

6. Research the Marketplace

The grass is not always greener on the other side. While your current situation may be untenable, it is not always better elsewhere. In fact, once you've investigated the marketplace and talked to others, you might find that, by comparison, you're sitting pretty. It may not be enough to keep you there, but this realization will broaden your perspective and determine your next steps.

7. Attend Regional and National Meetings

Interacting with others at a similar level in your profession and forming an informal support group can make all the difference in the world. "Misery loves and needs company" just as we enjoy the opportunity to talk about what is going well in our professional lives.

Attend professional meetings. In addition to the networking and job opportunities you'll often get the reinforcement you need. Spending the money to go to these meetings, even if your company does not send you, can be an important investment in your future.

Regardless of what you decide to do, your decision to stay must not only be based on the short term, but on the long term and your own professional timetable. You must assess whether or not the changes you can make in the short term can become long-term solutions leading to personal and professional fulfillment. Are you "applying a bandage" or are you performing "corrective surgery"? Are the solutions you've reached toward improving your situation doable and durable?

Again, be cautious not to let your decision to stay rest on the shoulders of others. Your decision needs to be rooted in your own personal and professional goals. Empower yourself with your decision and move forward, whether that means staying, leaving, or beginning the process of anticipating your separation.

Ask Yourself

Activity A

As mentioned in this chapter, your decision to stay or leave is not only based on the short term, but the long term and your own professional goals and timetable. With that in mind, create a professional timeline for yourself over a three-year period based on short-term, mid-term, and long-term goals. Is your present work environment going to help you achieve those goals, or is it standing in your way? If you choose to stay, what action steps can you take to achieve your goals? What are the time frames for monitoring success?

Activity B

Also make a list of the barriers that stand in the way of achieving success. For example, when was the last time there was restructuring within the organization? What promotions have occurred within the organization? Have women moved to greater positions of responsibility? Has there been an effort to create diversity in the workplace? Whatever you consider to be the barriers, evaluate whether they are short term or ongoing.

What incremental steps or strategies can you identify for dealing with them? Would moving to another office solve a personality issue with a colleague? Is it possible for you to be supervised by someone else, if supervision is an issue? Once you've identified the issues and possible solutions, you then have the tools to discuss them with the individual who can implement the changes or at minimum be your advocate.

4

Anticipating the Separation

"Two days to freedom. It's time to go. The tolerance level I had for the job is beginning to wane. My anger is gone. It's just being replaced with impatience."

I **knew it was time** to go even before I signed my last three-year contract. I knew it two years prior. Maybe even before that. Professionally, I hadn't been happy for a long time. Yet, the security, the salary, family responsibilities, pride, ego and, more than anything else, my anxiety of the unknown did not allow me to entertain such thoughts. What would it take for me to make that decision to separate?

I'd like to say that it was made in a vacuum, that I woke up one day and decided this was it. That was not the case. I decided to act on my desire to leave because, yes, I was psychologically ready, but also because I could see that if I didn't make that decision, it could ultimately be made for me, and I needed to take steps to plan my separation.

Face the Facts

In the classic *Dragnet* show, Jack Webb, when discussing a case with his partner, would say, "Just the facts, just the facts." In other words, don't confuse me with details, excuses, or rationalizations. We need to look at the facts. We need to assess our professional standing within the organization and how we are viewed by our colleagues, our staff, our board members, or our corporate partners and ourselves. Whether we think the assessment is correct or not is irrelevant, for the cliché "Perception is reality" will probably determine our future.

If I am the chief executive officer of an organization, I need to ask myself: How is this organization being perceived? I need to put myself in the chair of my board members, shareholders or stakeholders and take a read on the climate surrounding me. What is the overall view of me as the lead professional? I might not like the message, yet I must be honest with myself and put aside pride and ego in order to take the necessary steps toward separation.

Recently, a colleague of mine stated:

> In my case, the handwriting was on the wall. We were a fundraising organization, and we weren't raising adequate dollars. I could rationalize it from today to tomorrow, recounting the history of the community, blaming it on the demographics. It didn't matter. At the end of the day, I was the CEO of this organization, and the perception was that the raison d'etre of the organization was not being fulfilled. While my person-

al capital was high with many, the perception that the organization was not doing the job more and more was being projected on me. I could have laid blame (and I did privately), but if I was ultimately going to win the "personal goal of survival" I had to face the facts, define a strategy, and implement it.

The bottom line is, do you want to be **right** or do you want **to win the game**? If you want to win, then this is what you need to do.

Line Up Your Allies

Professional relationships are tricky regardless of what working environment you're in, whether it's as a salesperson in a department store, a junior partner in a law firm, or the corporate head of a company. In some instances professional relationships go beyond professional colleagues and also include volunteers and lay leaders who serve as members of boards, key committees, or community-related projects. This is particularly true in the non-profit sector when you are working alongside volunteers who very often become friends and social acquaintances. It is easy to get intimately involved with these individuals, but it's these same "friends" who are often members of your boards, who have to evaluate your performance and could be deciding your professional fate. Regardless of the setting, you need to apply a great deal of judgment in relationships, never losing sight of the multiple roles being performed. On the other hand, you have developed very special relationships with certain people in key positions, whether they are lay leaders or professional colleagues, and their positive feelings about you can be critical as you plan your separation.

I had often said to my president and two past presidents that if they sensed a mood among the board that my leadership was being questioned, would they let me know because that would give me the opportunity to make my decision on my own terms and create my own timetable. In other words, line up your allies. Know whom you can trust and with whom you can discuss your plans for separation. **Yet, heed the cardinal rule: the fewer people you engage in this discussion, the better.**

Analyze Your Financial Situation

Part of anticipating the separation is a realistic analysis of your financial situation. Ask yourself these critical questions:

- ❒ Do you have sufficient savings to weather six months to a year of unemployment?

- ❒ How long can you sustain your lifestyle on your savings?

- ❒ What are your ongoing obligations and support of your spouse and children?

- ❒ Do you have a clear understanding of any contract (if you're fortunate enough to have one), legal documents, or employment policies regarding the organization's obligation to you?

This last question is vitally important. **A complete review of your contract, personnel codes, or severance policies should be performed by an attorney or legal counsel.** This individual should not be formally affiliated with the organization. Putting aside the obvious problem of conflict of interest, it is always better to have someone advise you who does not have a vested interest in, or a skewed view of, your organization but brings an outsider's objectivity to the situation.

Yet, more than just an analysis of your current financial affairs, you also need to assess your financial needs and goals for the future. If the demands and complexities of your present career are part of what is pushing you to separate, are you willing and able to live on less? Is quality of life really more important then professional mobility or financial success? How will less money affect your quality of life? What are you willing to give up? While money may not be your primary motivation for working, it will become very clear that when money becomes an issue, your motivation for work and the ability to give your all to whatever you're doing are hampered.

One other factor that needs to be considered, particularly if your plan to leave is contingent on staying in the same geographical region, is whether or not you will have to sign a noncompete agreement related to the work you will be doing. For instance if you have been a fundraiser, you may be restricted in raising funds in a like organization or in the community where you are now working.

Engage Your Family in Your Discussion

The decision to separate cannot be made alone or in a vacuum, since what you are anticipating not only affects you, but also your spouse and children. If you're a man, it may be perceived to be the macho thing to take control, act, and then report out what you have done. This is not the way to go. Those closest to you should be part of the process. While you may want to spare them your heightened insecurity and anxiety, keeping them in the loop makes them feel more secure. Information provides clarity and leads to less inference making and distortions of reality. In addition, their insight and perspective could prove to be pivotal in making the right decisions. One caution: don't inundate them with details. Inform them at certain key points along the way.

Discussing my decision to leave with my daughter gave me great comfort. Having a 16-year old, I was very concerned about the possibility of taking her out of school. When I told her what I was making a career change that might involve a move, she made it clear to me that she would prefer to stay where she was until after her senior year, although her distress about moving was far less than I had speculated. After that conversation, I knew she would adjust. In fact, she said, "If it's New York or L.A., I could have my bags packed in five minutes." I was relieved.

Define and Refine Your Professional Goals

While you are anticipating your separation, begin in earnest the process of asking yourself what is it that you really want to do.

Although you may not have a definite idea, you should begin to visualize possible work environments that are the right match for you. One way of seeing if a particular work environment is for you is to shadow a friend or professional for a day or so to get an idea of what that job really entails. You may find that you are more enamored with the idea of being a president, an attorney, or a supervisor, rather than doing the work of one. If you find this is what you want to be and do, you can begin revising your resume to address those settings. We will discuss the resume in Chapter 8, but it is important to get a jump-start so that when you finally do separate you will have at your fingertips your most important tool.

Ask Yourself

Activity A

One of the key considerations in your decision to separate is your financial security upon leaving. Either independently or by scheduling a special session with your accountant or financial planner, develop a financial strategy and budget for your separation and life after separation. Make sure you include the following elements:

☐ The length of time and financial obligation the organization has agreed is entitled to you. In other words how many months' salary will they continue to pay? When will your benefits end?

☐ The savings you have accumulated for this very purpose.

☐ The length of time you can sustain the lifestyle to which you are accustomed.

☐ Your ongoing obligations and support for your spouse and children.

☐ Your ability to access credit, loans, or other financial transactions once you are no longer employed.

☐ An assessment of your pension plan, 401k, 403B, etc.

☐ Expenses incurred during a job search process or the establishment of your own business.

☐ Expenses related to relocation.

There will be other factors to consider, but the primary question that must be addressed is, how much time can you allow yourself for your job exploration, job placement, and job adjustment? All three of these phases will require financial resources and you need to be prepared.

Activity B

In addition to addressing very practical matters such as finances, you must also begin the process of addressing your feelings of self-worth and reflecting back in a very personal way on your accomplishments and successes, strengths and weaknesses. Engaging in this somewhat painful but mostly positive reflection will help you determine your professional goals for the future and how much risk you might be willing to take in pursuing a new job or a new career direction. The value of this process, however, is totally dependent on your willingness to be honest with yourself. If you are, you should ask yourself the following questions and write down the answers:

❏ When did you feel most proud of yourself both professionally and personally? The least proud? Describe.

❏ In what instances in your life have you taken the most risk, professionally and personally? The least risk?

❏ What motivated you to take those risks? Why didn't you take them?

❏ What behaviors did that risk-taking require?

❏ What were the results of taking those risks?

❏ What do you consider to be your "special power," as described in Sign #2, in Chapter 2? Why?

❏ Can you think of a job situation where this "special power" could be used to its maximum advantage?

❏ What is the one skill or competency you refuse to admit you don't own? Do you need it to move to the next job or career? Can you acquire that skill now?

In answering these questions, what conclusions have you drawn? Write them down so you can reflect on them. Do they give you a clearer picture of what your career goals should be?

5

Moving Forward

*"Is this the best time to leave? Should I wait or should
I do it now? Politically, is this the best time? I've never
been so ambivalent in my life."*

Once you have read the signs and anticipated
your separation, it is now time to take the appropriate steps and move forward. The worst thing
you can do is to do nothing. Indecision can be paralyzing and
will ultimately consume opportunity for change and reinforce a
sense of "valuelessness." If not now, when? With this in mind,
the following steps need to be taken.

Make the Timing Right

I don't know who said it, but one of the cultural axioms we probably agree to is that timing is everything. In my own separation
process and in conversations with colleagues over many years,
this has certainly been the case. This sense of timing has two
dimensions: (1) your personal timetable and (2) the organizational and political timetable. While we have discussed your
personal timetable based on the signs identified in Chapter 2, it

is critical that the timing be right and strategic regarding the **organization**. You need to ask the following questions:

Is the leadership of the organization in a state of transition? This is vitally important. You want to make sure that your allies, those individuals who will support you, are still in power and can make decisions in your behalf.

Is the organization reaching a critical level or pivotal moment in its growth and development? If the organization is moving to the next phase of growth and development, this may be an ideal time for you to separate, particularly if you can be credited with helping it to reach its current state. Your personal legacy to the organization is very important, for it will be a vital asset in helping you achieve your next career goals.

In retrospect, it might have been better if I had left my organization earlier. I had accomplished what many believed to be the impossible. I had taken two nonprofit organizations with their respective accumulation of history, culture, and egos on both the lay and professional sides and had put them together. Perhaps I should have said, "Gary Rubin, wrap it up in a nice big bow, claim victory, and move on. Don't try to beat the odds." The chance of a CEO surviving the merger or consolidation of two prior organizations is a statistical downslide. I'm not so sure it's even a good idea, for no matter how solid that CEO is, there will always be baggage based on what people think they know about the inside person versus a person from the outside.

Putting that digression aside, in your decision to leave, the concept of **legacy** is an important one, not only for institutional memory but also in a very personal way in helping you assess your professional self-worth and evaluating your skills and accomplishments. Even if you've never thought of your record of achievement in a business or organization in terms of "my legacy," all of us, no matter what jobs we're in, have accumulated a record of achievement. What set of skills made you successful in the job you are considering leaving? Do you have the skills to move to something else? For example, can the healer also be a hard-nosed manager, or does it take two different types of people with different skill sets.

Identify What You Want and Need in the Separation

As I stated earlier, it is very important that you have a clear idea of what you must have and are entitled to in separating. Again, make sure the elements of your separation or severance agreement are clear and have been fully reviewed by an attorney or legal counsel. You must be certain that all ambiguities are anticipated and addressed prior to formal discussions. There will be a temptation, almost a blind spot, not to deal with certain questions or details because you just want it to be over. Don't be stupid. Don't be seduced by the euphoria you are experiencing by having made the decision to leave. Ask the hard questions. Have those points resolved now, even if it takes a little longer. After the deed is done and the papers are signed, you will not be able to go back, nor will that be your desire. Therefore, make a list and check it twice.

Set a Date for Your Announcement

Once you have taken care of the above details, you and your leadership have a clear idea of what you need and want, the waters have been tested as much as possible on the acceptance of those terms, and your allies are all lined up to be your advocates and spokespersons, then and only then can you make your intentions more widely known. This may be more complex in the nonprofit environment where the approval process for reaching closure on these decisions is longer and involves more people. In stating your intentions to your stakeholders, make sure you are careful of the language you use. Check this out with your attorney. You may even want to have this scripted, for there is no room for misinterpretation. For instance, what words do you want to use to describe what it is you are doing? Are you **leaving, resigning,** or **separating** from the organization? The words you use not only affect the public relations element of your decision, but also could affect the severance you might receive.

Be in Control

The key word here is **control**. You want to control as much of the situation as possible, and two requirements for control are **consistency** and **timing**. Make sure you are conveying a consistent message. It is vital that family members, key employees, or any other individuals who will be answering questions about your departure are on the same page. While this is easier to control if you have access to a formal public relations division within your organization, it's more difficult with individuals.

If you wish to control what appears in the media about you, you can assign a person as the official spokesperson for speaking on your decision. On the other hand, you may decide that this person should be you and no one else. In addition, you want to make sure you inform key groups of people as quickly as possible with your version of reality. With the availability of e-mail, faxes, etc., crafting a message from you as quickly as possible preempts a lot of conjecture and false perceptions. Remember, everyone is going to know anyway, so why not tell them the way you want to tell them? Immediacy is key. News travels fast and people will be saying "God bless you" before you even sneeze.

Deal With the Press

"The press is still trying to find a story here. Why am I so concerned about this? I just don't want anything to be cast in a negative light. I just want to end this chapter." This plaintive remark may not apply to everyone. Most of us leave our jobs unnoticed by the outside world, for we are not in a public position that will capture the attention of the press. However, for some high-ranking individuals making a change, this will be an added dimension to address. If this is the case for you, consider the advice below. If not, you may want to jump ahead to Activity A in "Ask Yourself" on page 53.

If you have been in a high-profile position, the press will be looking for the story behind the story regarding your departure.

The following guidelines will help you handle this to your advantage:

1. **Anticipate their need to know**. Recognize that the press will be contacting you and others to discuss your decision. Make sure you have lined up individuals they can speak to, but first ensure all of you tell the same story. Remember, a consistent message is of critical importance.

2. **Use the press to your advantage and develop a press release**. Again, craft a message that will not only set the record straight but can be a positive advertisement for you, particularly if you are seeking another position. In the best of worlds, the press release that you develop would be sent out to numerous outlets prior to the development of their own story and that's what would be printed.

3. **When talking to the press, remember (with some exceptions) you are always on the record**. Nothing you say will be kept in confidence. Everything you say is part of the record. When talking to a reporter, don't feel you have to fill space with words. Speak in measured, thoughtful language, remembering all the time that your hesitation or your pausing will not be picked up in print. Also, there is nothing wrong with saying "No comment."

Ask Yourself

Activity A

For those who won't be dealing with the press, you still may want to make your "own statement" to your co-workers upon your departure. Depending on the circumstances, you may feel taking out an ad in the organization newsletter or publication to thank colleagues might be appropriate. With that in mind, create an ad for your departure. If you were a supervisor or division head, is there a way to thank people in addition to using the ad as an opportunity to remind people of the achievements that happened on your watch?

Activity B

If you have been in a high-profile or public position, the press will be looking for "the rest of the story." Therefore, take control and develop your own press release for your departure. Include in this release an overview of your accomplishments as well as the positive legacy you are leaving behind. Here is an example to help you:

> John Doe, president of the World Youth Organization since 1995, has decided to leave his post, effective January 1, 2003. After serving WYO for over seven years, Doe is looking for other challenging opportunities to utilize his skills and expertise. He called his years at WYO extremely gratifying both personally and professionally.

During his watch as president, Doe, who prior to this position served as vice-president of the United Kingdom Division of WYO, was a driving force in the consolidation of the North American offices of WYO and those of the United Kingdom. Harrison Collier, past international president of WYO notes, "To be a part of John Doe's planning, processing, and implementation of the consolidation process was inspiring."

Sherry London, president of Leadership Forward, a private foundation which supports WYO, reflects on Doe's departure, "I am sad that he is leaving. John is an exemplary leader and has been a major force in the heightened credibility and profile of the organization."

Since the consolidation, many accomplishments have resulted, including the significant growth of the WYO foundation from $50 million to $125 million in assets and the establishment of the Global Youth Awards Program, which identifies and recognizes outstanding youth from all over the world and provides scholarships for recipients to attend top-tier institutions worldwide."

Former president of WYO, Stuart Mellancamp, says, "John's departure leaves a lasting legacy of service and commitment that only bodes well for the organization's future vitality."

Doe said that WYO should be proud of its impressive history and, with the continued support and enlistment of key professional and volunteer leadership, WYO should reach new heights and move further toward maximizing the potential of youth around the world.

6

Taking Action

*"I don't want to leave my office carting off boxes like
some fugitive from the IRS."*

There is no question that once you make your
decision to leave and the sequence of events
already discussed have taken place, the "lame-duck
syndrome" will begin. It's just the natural course of events. That
is why it is important to schedule your departure date as close
as possible to your public announcement. Also, it is very important that you have a date in mind that can be announced when
you let the public know your decision. This way, it will appear
that your departure is in **your** control and not in the control of
the organization, even if the latter is the case.

It is also important, as difficult as it can be in some instances,
to maintain the structured decorum and authority of your position
for the duration of your tenure. Again, impression management
is critical, and you want people to know this is **your** decision.
Don't let anger or harsh words taint your record as a professional. You've withstood the negativity, if that's the case, for this
long. You can take it a little longer. Also, you want to make sure
that you leave the organization having done all you could to

maintain organizational stability until your departure. Let everyone think **you're** the martyr, the one with integrity rather than leave them with an impression of you as an angry individual slamming the door behind you.

Finally, the cliché "Don't burn any bridges" must be adhered to above all else. Your anger and lashing out at individuals or the organization might make you feel good in the short term but will have damaging effects in the long term. Besides, your reactions are being skewed by the immediacy of the situation, the myriad emotions you are experiencing, and your fear of the unknown. While you may feel that you have an accurate perspective on your situation at this moment in time, that perspective will change as you have the benefit of some distance and detatchment. What will not change, nor can they be erased, are the comments or views you may have expressed in the heat of anger.

Also, those same individuals who may have been the object of your wrath and emotion might, believe it or not, be an ally or a support for you in the future. Professional situations very often create strange bedfellows. It may sound ludicrous, but in a world where the fate of organizations and the fate of professionals are increasingly changing and fluid, your current opponent could be your partner at a future time. This notion should not be looked upon negatively but perhaps as a the reality of doing business. Also, the way you handle a difficult situation, leaving an organization with grace and dignity, can be your ticket to your next position.

No Dramatic Departures

Regardless of the circumstances, you should maintain your dignity and class until the end. You don't want to imply that you're leaving in the middle of the night like a tax fugitive from the IRS, carrying boxes and personal belongings to your car at the eleventh hour. Instead, once you've chosen to leave, begin taking a little more out of your office each day. By the time of your effective date, you'll have completed your move. It all will appear seamless with little acrimony and a minimum of drama.

To Party or Not to Party

That is the question! Certainly, there will be individuals within the organization, staff, and lay leaders who will want to give you the proverbial going-away party. Your immediate response, depending on the circumstances, may be to say no. On reflection, however, there are several reasons to say yes! First, your departure from the organization is not something that only you have been dealing with, but also those who have worked with you. There may even be a sense of loss or grief in your leaving, particularly with individuals who have worked by your side, such as your secretary or administrative assistant. You need to be less self-centered in this instance and give them an opportunity for closure.

Second, parties or tributes help to offset rumors about why you're leaving even under the best of circumstances. Third, they may also provide you or one of your associates the forum to reflect on all of your accomplishments and allow those present the opportunity to see the legacy of achievement you are leaving behind. Your next job or career opportunity could be stimulated by that review.

Ask Yourself

Activity

In light of the above, if you had to give a hypothetical testimonial speech in honor of yourself, what would you say? Include the following elements:

❐ Achievements

❐ Character of the person

❐ Legacy

7

Starting Your New Journey

"This could be a very exciting chapter in my life if only
I would get a grip and not get caught up in what
everyone is thinking."

FREE AT LAST! FREE AT LAST! It will seem euphoric at first. The idea of waking up every day and not having a particular place to go will be liberating. You will catch yourself beginning to worry about something and then realizing you don't need to worry about that anymore. On the other hand, there will almost be a void. You've gotten used to worrying. It even had a certain comfort level for you. It was predictable. You don't really know how to deal with life without worry. However, don't fret. Old worries will be replaced with new ones as you begin your new adventure.

The first steps in charting your course are very important.

Give Yourself Permission

Take some time to decompress. Depending on your financial circumstances, you may want to take a few weeks vacation or longer to detox emotionally and psychologically from your previous situation. You need to take the time **now** even if it's relatively short. You need to give yourself the permission to do nothing for a while. It's truly okay. Immediate psychological separating will not be easy. You'll still be reaching for the phone or waiting for it to ring. The first realization you'll experience after a week or so is that the phone won't ring. You're history, and it's okay. You don't want to be involved in the organization once you've left it. Why get aggravated about things that are no longer in your control, and which you're not going to be able to change?

Therefore, enjoy your new freedom, and the first step in doing that is to do nothing for a while. If you can't afford the vacation, do other things. Go to the beach or the movies in the middle of the day. Go out to dinner on a night when you would have had a board meeting or an appointment with a client. Reward yourself because you deserve it!

Use this newfound freedom to make other changes in your life. Pick up your daughter from school or take her to school in the morning. Take your spouse out to dinner just by yourselves. Join a health club and work out a few mornings a week. Use this monumental change in you professional life as an opportunity to make some transformational changes in your personal life. If nothing else, you might lose a few pounds.

Establish a Base of Operations

Once you have had adequate time to emotionally separate from your previous situation and you are ready to begin a new chapter in your life, it's very important to have someplace to go in the morning, a **center of gravity** if you will, as you begin your job exploration or your new venture.

Remember, during all of those years of working you had an office to go to, and without that you may feel as if you are in a state of limbo, not anchored to anything or anyone. You may want to affiliate yourself with an outplacement firm. In addition to helping you design a resume, some also provide you with a physical office and secretarial services. However, this is not always necessary. Designating a room in your house as an office might serve you just as well. Making this space more job-oriented will help.

1. Create an Office

Identify a space in your home or garage that has minimal access by everyone else, particularly during the day when much of your activity will take place.

Create an office-like atmosphere. Surround the room with things that make you feel confident and proud of your past accomplishments, all those things that make you feel worthy or remind you that you are a person of value and achievement. The plaques, citations, and significant photographs that you may have put in a drawer before should now be prominently displayed. You want a space that reinforces your successes every time you enter. Whether you admit it or not, depending on the circumstances of your departure, your ego is somewhat fragile and you need that "psychological lift."

Any change you've made, even if you've orchestrated it, can create some anxiety. Being reminded of your abilities can be comforting. Your surroundings have a lot to do with creating that comfort level.

2. Structure and Organization

Make sure your new workstation, whatever form it takes, is structured and organized. All the personal chaos you may be facing can be buffeted by the organization and control you have in this new space. The space doesn't have to be elaborate. A closet, even a portion of a closet in that room, can be useful in storing resumes, stationery, and reference materials or whatever you need to function as a professional.

Once you've identified your workspace, make sure that you have the essential professional tools to begin your new "world of work." Below is a list of professional tools that will help you get started. Check off the ones you already have and consider those you still need.

3. Professional Tools

It is extremely important that while you are in a state of limbo that you not appear as if you are in a state of limbo. You want to create, as much as possible, a professional presence. Some very minimal items at little expense can do this for you:

Computers and Laptops

More than likely you already have a computer or laptop at your disposal, but if you don't, it is an absolute must. Your job search will be severely hampered if you do not have computer access. If you presently have no computer access and will be purchasing a computer, you might consider the advantages of a laptop which will give you portability whether you are searching for career information at a library or keeping up with your e-mails or correspondence when you are out of town.

Not having computer access will affect your personal credibility. Just like your address and phone number, in the 21st century work world your e-mail address is part of who you are. Without an e-mail identity or computer capability, you could find yourself out of the game or easily dismissed as someone who is behind the times, and not "with it." The once held attitude of "I don't need all that, I like talking to people, not computers" just doesn't cut it anymore.

It certainly doesn't cut it in your job search, for, in some instances, search firms as well as potential employers will not accept your resume in hard copy but will require you to send it to them online. In addition, your daily communication and information gathering for job openings, as well as general networking, will be stymied at the outset without computer access.

In addition to a computer or a laptop, you may want to consider investing in a printer and a scanner for the ability to make quality copies of resumes, proposals, or any other support material that will give you additional advantage in the job market.

Business Cards and Personalized Stationary

In today's world, everyone is always asking, "Can I have your card?" While you may no longer have an appropriate business card to hand them, you can, at a minimum, hand them a calling card. The card would have your name, street address, e-mail address, and phone, mobile, and fax numbers; it would also include your academic or professional degrees. It allows you an even exchange. You ask for the card and they for yours. If you feel compelled to have something on the card, use the word consultant. Anyone can be a consultant. Aren't they already?

Like business cards, personalized stationary is a fundamental tool in establishing your new professional identity. Again, it does not have to be elaborate or costly. In fact, less is more. A standard white or cream colored linen paper provides you with the professional image you want without screaming out for attention. Make sure your stationary and business cards are coordinated and match in style, quality, and design.

Voice Mail

For the last eight years, I did not have voice mail on my home phone because I did not want to feel obligated to return calls after work hours, particularly since work hours in my profession had no limits, no beginning or end. Now, voice mail is an absolute must. It is critically important for individuals to be able to leave you messages. Activate voice mail on your primary phone as well as on your mobile phone. (Yes, a mobile phone, discussed below, is an absolute necessity.) Like everything else, the whole thing is timing, and any barriers that do not allow others to be in touch with you can result in a missed opportunity.

Fax Machines and Copiers

We can no longer say "The check is in the mail" any more than we can say "I'll mail you a resume." More and more, you will find a fax machine to be a critical element in your job search. Many fax machines are a combination fax and copier. While you can probably go to any office supply store or post office to fax or copy something, there is nothing better than to be able to do it at your convenience and with confidentiality. If you want to fax a resume to the West Coast, being able to do so during that three-hour time difference can be a determining factor. One other tip: Get a separate line for your fax machine so you're not competing with your telephone or computer.

E-mail

In today's job search world, more and more communication takes place by e-mail. Employers often prefer receiving resumes and letters by e-mail rather than by mail or fax.

Indeed, the fax is increasingly becoming obsolete in today's electronic job search world. Be sure you know how to format and transmit your resume and letters by e-mail. For starters, see Joyce Lain Kennedy's latest edition of **Resumes for Dummies** (John Wiley & Sons, 2003) and Susan Britton Whitcomb's and Pat Kendall's **e-Resumes** (McGraw-Hill, 2001).

Cell Phones and Pagers

Did you ever notice that when a cell phone starts ringing in a restaurant or a movie theater, at least half the audience starts jostling in their seats looking for their phones?

The reality is that practically everyone has a cell phone today or at least has access to one. When picking my daughter up from her high school, and watching the students stream out of the building, I noticed that two out of three seemed to be juggling their backpacks and their car keys to make that very important call on their cell phones. In newscasts of Third World countries with devastation in the background you see the residents with their cell phones at their ear.

As someone who must now compete in a world where everything moves more quickly and opportunity may knock very briefly, you must do all you can to be available, be contacted, and make the connection. If you don't think this is true all you have to do is look back on your own experiences in hiring personnel. I'm sure you can recall a situation where there were two candidates equally qualified for a position. You needed to fill it, you made two calls, and one answered and one didn't or couldn't be reached. You hired the one that did. Granted, depending on the circumstances, you might try the call again, but the point being made is an obvious one. As a past professor of mine used to say, "If you're not there, you're wrong." The same case can be made for the use of pagers, although not as strongly as for cell phones.

Electronic Calendars

I've never been a gadget person, but I find myself more and more slowly letting technology creep into my life. When I left my last position, my staff gave me a Palm Pilot as a going-away gift. For months it sat in my newly created office unopened. It was a struggle enough just to acclimate myself to my computer (which up until that point had not been used too frequently), my cell phone, and voice mail. Yet now that I'm using it and learning how to use it more effectively everyday, like anything else, I wonder what I did without it. Don't get me wrong, I haven't totally given up my daytimer, but I now leave that in the car. The Palm Pilot is a lot more impressive when I'm sitting at Starbucks.

Ask Yourself

Activity

At the beginning of this chapter, I talked about using your professional change as an opportunity to examine other aspects of your life and to pursue activities you had neglected or didn't get around to previously. This can be helpful in getting you to decompress before you begin your job exploration. Remember, you deserve it. They might fall into the following categories:

❒ Hobbies you've wanted to pursue

❒ Continuing education

❒ Reconnecting with old friends

❒ Family time

❒ Travel

Create a top-ten list of things you want to do during your "decompression phase." Select one that can be done and completed in the short term and one that can be pursued over the long term.

8

The Most Important Tool—
The Resume

*"How do you capsulize 30 year of personal and life
experience in a couple of pages?"*

It has become Hollywood legend that during one lean point in her career, actress Bette Davis placed an ad in the paper advertising her availability for a job. It obviously worked, for some of her premier roles came afterwards. Yet, one of the reasons it worked was that she had a celluloid resume that could speak to her accomplishments and her extraordinary talent. Still, even Bette had to market it.

One of the key elements in marketing yourself is the development of a resume. While there are many books that deal with this more thoroughly than I will do here, there are five lessons I have learned in my own journey:

1. Have several versions of your resume so that you can target a particular audience or employer.

You should tailor your resume to each potential employer so that you can emphasize those aspects of your experience that have particular relevance to them. Sometimes this can be achieved in the cover letter that accompanies your resume, but there is no question that tailoring your resume to a specific organization is that much more impressive—and more effective.

This does not mean that you change the content (and certainly not the facts), but you may want to change the emphasis or focus. At a minimum, you need both a chronological resume and a functional resume. **Chronological resumes** are most useful if you want a position similar to the one you're in presently or at least in a similar environment, for they focus the reader on your most recent career experience. They are not as effective if you want to change work environments or careers. These kinds of changes will necessitate a resume that projects the leadership and character traits that have brought you achievement and success. The **functional resume**, emphasizing major accomplishments, will be more effective in helping you achieve this objective. Individuals who have a life time of work experience and want to emphasize what they can do based on past experience yet want to deemphasize their age or chronology will find this type of resume more appropriate.

With regard to age, while most employers will stay away from directly asking your age (they shouldn't be asking) they are thinking about it nonetheless, and you want to redirect them to focus on your achievements. Hopefully, they will draw the conclusion that it is your significant work experience that makes you so valuable. The functional resume helps to convey this.

2. **Whatever kind of resume or format you use, you need to show a record of achievement and success.**

   Be as specific as possible. Quantify and qualify specific job experiences. Don't get caught in the trap of platitudes and general statements. You don't have to tell all in a resume, but you want the reader to be enticed enough to call you in for an interview or to take the next step.

3. **Less is definitely more.**

   While there is a great deal of discussion (believe it or not, people actually debate these things) on the appropriate length of a resume—some experts would say one page for every ten years—it is clear that the **less pages, the better.** Potential employers want to "get the picture" as quickly as possible.

   As someone who hired numerous individuals over the years, the last thing I wanted to do was to plow through a 30-page resume. The resume is not a "curriculum vitae," and should tell your story quickly and concisely. While you may be tempted to tell everything in your resume, leave something for the interview. Remember, a resume is nothing more than a marketing tool.

4. **What you don't want is your resume to result in the "Is of Identity Syndrome."**

   What I mean by this is that very often we assume a person can only perform a certain range of activities based on a job description or title. For instance, Adele has been a secretary. Therefore, that means that she can type, use the computer, and answer the phone. In fact, Adele can do many other things based on skills and experiences she has accumulated over a lifetime of work, but we assume because of her present title and position she can only perform a finite set of tasks. This is another reason why the functional resume may be preferable. Functional resumes more easily show **transferable skills** that can be valuable for a variety of positions.

People—often headhunters or job recruiters—will want to put you in a box, categorize you as one kind of person with one type of expertise. You don't want to fall into this trap. More than likely, you can do many things and have many different kinds of skills. While you want to highlight those skills and experiences which have brought you much of your success, you also want to project your versatility and your marketability in areas outside of your present work environment or career history.

5. **In describing your experience, you need to choose language that conveys confidence and the level of your responsibility.**

Descriptors need to be active rather than passive. Using action words like supervised, managed, and coordinated will help the potential employer see the application of your experience to a variety of settings. For example, saying you led the organization to record levels of sales in the 2001-2002 fiscal year is very different than saying you were part of a team that accomplished a given task. Developing a resume is not the time to be overly modest about your achievements (provided they are true).

Ask Yourself

Activity

Remember, resumes are just marketing tools. They do not have to tell the entire story. All they need to do is create enough interest so that, as famed commentator Paul Harvey used to say, you have the opportunity to "tell the rest of the story." However, in order to do this, your resume must not only convey your experiences and accomplishments effectively but must be focused on a particular position.

To see if there is a match between your resume and your professional goals, develop your ideal job description. Would your resume get you the job? What about the job qualifications not reflected in your resume? What can be strengthened? Once you have completed this exercise, search the Internet and other job sources to see if there is such a job available. If there is, why not apply?

Recommended Resources

Books

The following books represent some of the best resources for writing and distributing resumes and letters:

201 Dynamite Job Search Letters, 4th Edition, Ron and Caryl Krannich (Impact Publications, 2001)

Asher's Bible of Executive Resumes, Donald Asher (Ten Speed Press, 1996)

Best Cover Letters for $100,000+ Jobs, Wendy S. Enelow (Impact Publications, 2002)

Best Resumes and CVs for International Jobs, Ronald L. Krannich and Wendy S. Enelow (Impact Publications, 2002)

Best Resumes for $100,000+ Jobs, Wendy S. Enelow (Impact Publications, 2002)

Cover Letters for Dummies, 2nd Edition, Joyce Lain Kennedy (John Wiley & Sons, 2000) *e-Resumes,* Susan Britton Whitcomb and Pat Kendall (McGraw-Hill, 2001)

Haldane's Best Cover Letters for Professionals, Bernard Haldane Associates (Impact Publications, 1999)

Haldane's Best Resumes for Professionals, Bernard Haldane Associates (Impact Publications, 1999)

High Impact Resumes and Letters, 8th Edition, Ronald L. Krannich and William J. Banis (Impact Publications, 2003)

Resume Catalog: 200 Damn Good Examples, Yana Parker (Ten Speed Press, 1996)

Resumes for Dummies, 4th Edition, Joyce Lain Kennedy (John Wiley & Sons, 2003)

Resumes That Knock 'Em Dead, Martin Yate (Adams Media, 2002)

Sure-Hire Resumes, Robbie Miller Kaplan (Impact Publications, 1998)

Websites

The following websites provide assistance in writing and distributing resumes:

Online Resume Tips

- Monster.com   resume.monster.com
- America's CareerInfoNet   www.acinet.org/acinet
- JobStar   jobstar.org/tools/resume
- CareerBuilder   careerbuilder.com
- Quintessential Careers   quintcareers.com
- Wetfeet   wetfeet.com
- Jobsonline   jobsonline.com
- WinningTheJob   www.winningthejob.com

Professional Resume Writer Groups

- Professional Association of Resume Writers
  and Career Coaches   www.parw.com
- Professional Resume Writing
  and Research Association   prwra.com
- National Resume Writers' Association   nrwa.com
- NetWorker
  Career Services   careercatalyst.com/resume.htm

Online Resume Writing Services

- A&A Resume   aandaresume.com

- A-Advanced Resume Service   topsecretresumes.com

- Advanced Career Systems   resumesystems.com

- Advanced Resumes   advancedresumes.com

- Advantage Resume   advantageresume.com

- Best Fit Resumes   bestfitresumes.com

- Cambridge Resume Service   cambridgeresume.com

- Career Resumes   career-resumes.com

- CertifiedResumeWriters   certifiedresumewriters-.com

- eResume (Rebecca Smith's)   eresumes.com

- e-resume.net   e-resume.net

- Executiveagent.com   executiveagent.com

- Free-Resume-Tips   free-resume-tips.com

- Impact Resumes   impactresumes.com

- Leading Edge Resumes   leadingedgeresumes.com

- Resume Agent   resumeagent.com

- Resume.com   resume.com

- Resume Creators   resumecreators.com

- ResumeMaker   resumemaker.com

- Resume Writer   resumewriter.com

- WSACORP.com   www.wsacorp.com

Resume Blasting Services (be careful what you pay for!)

- BlastMyResume — blastmyresume.com
- CareerPal — careerpal.com
- Careerxpress.com — careerxpress.com
- E-cv.com — e-cv.com
- Executiveagent.com — executiveagent.com
- HotResumes — hotresumes.com
  (posts to multiple job boards)
- Job Search Page — jobsearchpage.com
  (international focus)
- Job Village — jobvillage.com
- Nrecruiter.com — nrecruiter.com
- ResumeBlaster — resumeblaster.com
- Resume Booster — resumebooster.com
- ResumeBroadcaster — resumebroadcaster.com
- Resume Path — resumepath.com
- ResumeZapper — resumezapper.com
- ResumeXpress — resumexpress.com
- RocketResume — rocketresume.com
- See Me Resumes — seemeresumes.com
- Your Missing Link — yourmissinglink.com
- WSACORP.com — www.wsacorp.com

9

Beginning Your Search

"The arrogance of search firms. Don't they know who I am?"

The question of where to begin may at first seem overwhelming. However, you will find almost immediately, if you have been unhappy long enough, that you have been thinking about this process, and you have already narrowed down the areas you want to pursue professionally. While you may not have a clear job objective, you probably know what you *don't* want to do and where you *don't* want to be working. Once you have your professional tools in place, your resumes completed, you can begin your search process. I have found the following steps to be most helpful.

Reconnect and Network

While networking is usually focused on meeting people you don't know and developing relationships, reconnecting focuses on people from your past whom, in many instances, you haven't seen in a long time. Both of these activities are critical elements in your job exploration.

81

Reconnect

When you think back on your life, there are probably a number of instances that stand out, whether they were in a work setting, volunteer setting, or personal situation, where you felt particularly good about yourself and others saw you in the same light. Perhaps it was the way you solved a problem, completed a task, gave advice, attained a goal, or demonstrated a certain talent. Regardless of the circumstances, you were in control and others looked at you as a person who could get the job done, be depended upon, or provide leadership. Reflecting back on those instances and the individuals who appreciated and admired your talent, your skill, or your kindness, could those individuals be of help to you now? At minimum they would want to see you again, for their memory of you is rooted in such a positive experience from the past.

I often think back on a comment that someone made about me, unaware that I had heard it. Walking into a restaurant one day, I saw someone I had known and who had come to me for advice and counsel many years earlier. After an exchange of greetings and an introduction to the person who was with him, I started walking away to my table. As I did, I heard my acquaintance say to his friend, "That guy is really a successful person." Unfortunately for my ego, I could not hear the rest of his comments, but his description of me as a "successful person" has stuck with me and given me a lot of confidence over the years. Why not reconnect with such persons from your past? In my case I did and it helped lead me to my current success. While you certainly can check the phonebook or old address books that you have been keeping for years to find a particular contact, a more reliable way of obtaining updated addresses and phone numbers is to click on various websites which are dedicated to this. (See "Online Locators," page 97.)

Reconnecting with individuals from various stages of your personal and professional life can have tremendous benefits. Past associations, such as alumni groups, boards, committees, jobs, and volunteer experiences, can provide a treasure-trove of possible contacts for job and career opportunities as well as making you feel good. In your current state of mind, you may only be focusing on negative feelings about yourself based on your most recent work experience and questioning your talent and the way others saw you in that setting. Why not reconnect with individuals who saw you only as a success? Don't underestimate the power of positive energy you receive from others to move you forward.

In addition, just as you have changed over the years and have developed professionally, so have these individuals. They may now be in exactly the right position to help someone whom they admired or who helped them in the past. That someone is **you**.

Network

"Strike when the iron is hot" is particularly relevant in networking and reconnecting. When you announced your decision to leave (if you even made an announcement) or told others you were leaving, you may have received a flurry of calls from individuals sharing their thoughts with you. A few might even have offered their help and assistance in getting you another position—a few. As the weeks and months go by, you will receive even less, if any, of those random calls. You will need to make it happen yourself. Remember, no one cares as much about your career as you do. Therefore you need to connect with as many people as you can, and keep the momentum going. The worst thing you can do is hide and "go underground." Hiding will only add to the rumor mill regarding your departure if you were in a public position and even if you weren't, the longer you hide, the more difficult it will be to begin again.

Depending on who you are, what position you held, and the circumstances of your departure, you may be considered a hot commodity and you should take advantage of this "temporary status." This will not last long. However, most of us do not have that advantage and must seek out our own connections and distinguish ourselves from the numerous others who are searching the marketplace. On a more practical side, you want to avoid huge gaps in your resume. You can probably explain a year, but beyond that you become somewhat questionable. Saying you were a consultant during that gap will only play so well, unless you really were.

You will also find that the more people you talk to, the greater your perspective, and the more you will see that the stress and insecurity you are feeling and experiencing is normal. Discovering this is very therapeutic, for there will be down days and moments of anxiety as you begin your search.

While you want to see as many people as possible, your list should fall primarily into three categories:

1. People who have made major career changes successfully

2. People who are successful

3. People who can help you focus on your specific career goal

People Who Made Successful Career Changes

Talk to individuals who have made successful career changes, particularly those from your profession. In addition to getting support for what you're doing and reinforcement in the end result, it will help you identify environments that you didn't know existed that can use your talents. Also, someone who has made a successful change will be glad to give advice (it's flattering). Even if you don't know these individuals, others do and they may help you connect with them.

In addition, read the newspapers, local magazines, and community newsletters that feature success stories of individuals who have made life and career changes. People who have done this will be the most empathic to your situation and you may find that even a "cold call" might result in setting up an informational interview, an interview where you are not asking for a job but simply getting a perspective on a particular career or work environment.

People Who are Successful

In addition to talking to people like yourself from a similar profession, why not talk to those individuals who have been uniquely successful in whatever they've chosen to do? What has driven them in times of adversity? How have they managed to cope in difficult circumstances? How did they land on their feet? Also, successful people know other successful people. You want to talk to **winners** (not defined by financial success)—people who have achieved their personal and professional goals. Of course, when you talk to these individuals you will find they have their own demons, and your perception of them might be very different than their own. In either case, conversations with them will reinforce your own worth, help you realize your fears and anxieties are not unique, and you might even learn some of their secrets of success which can get you closer to your next job or career.

People Who can Help You Focus on Your Own Career Goals

The third group of individuals is comprised of those who force you to take a reality check. It is very easy to become hypnotized by the process of searching without ever really coming to grips with what you ultimately need to do. Eventually, that severance package or your financial reserve will come to an end and that state of total liberation will disappear. There will be a day of decision. While the lunch meetings with people in the first two categories will be helpful in getting you to think, dream, and set your direction, this third group of individuals will help you sort things out, analyze your options, and bring you back to reality. They will be the ones to say, "Gary, get real." These are the realists. They might be as close to you as a spouse, or they could be your accountant or a past business associate. Regardless of who they are, you will resist talking to these people. They are not always going to say what you want to hear, but you need to hear them, for they will balance the other voices

Search Firms

Don't be surprised or offended if you note a degree of arrogance when dealing with search firms, particularly the larger or more corporate-oriented ones. Remember, they are not working for you. They are working for their clients. In fact, in most instances, they will never meet you but simply pass on your resume (provided the computer identified it as a match) to an interested client.

Having said that, search firms—and there are various kinds— can be of great assistance. However, don't be seduced into thinking that they will do the work for you and all you need to do is sit idly by and respond to the opportunities. "I have my resumes on file, on the Internet, and God will provide." While they can be helpful, and I recommend affiliating yourself with several, for people do get positions from working with them, chances are the job you ultimately land will be a result of your own networking and reconnecting process.

Develop a Search Plan

Set goals and have a plan for your job search and think about the following as you begin your exploration:

1. **Be in the right frame of mind.** You need to look at your job search as if it were a job and behave accordingly, particularly if you're at home or using your home as your office. Your psychological headset for your exploration is critically important.

2. **Set your alarm** like you would any other workday even though it may be set a little later, and structure your day. View it as if you're going to the office. And, you are. It's just that your office is at home.

3. **Get dressed.** While you may dress a bit more casually, particularly since "dress casual" has become more or less the norm, you want to have a professional presence even if you're in your home. Don't sit around in your pajamas or your robe and slippers. Your professional sense of yourself is critical in setting the tone for your day. It will even affect your responses on the phone. Also, you want to be ready at a moment's notice if you get a call and have an unexpected appointment.

4. **Do what you normally do** in any work setting. Make your lists, prioritize, and set your appointments for your day and your week. Log everything you do. Keep a list of your

appointments and a record of letters sent and received. Keep summary notes and follow-up steps to every appointment and meeting.

5. **Making phone calls** to individuals whom you don't know can produce anxiety. Make sure these calls are made from a position of power or confidence. What does that mean? It means sitting in a hardback chair or desk chair that psychologically gives you an air of confidence versus sitting on a couch or in an armchair. The position of "power" will vary from individual to individual, but your psyche when making these calls is significant. Nonverbal communication comes in many forms. The paralinguistic aspects of language—inflection, pitch, rate of speech—are transmitted to the person on the other end of the call. You can tell when a person is being rushed on the phone or whether that person is smiling, even though you can't see the person. Frame of mind is extremely important when you make those calls. So position yourself to communicate positive nonverbal messages.

6. **Setting appointments** on your own personal calendar or keeping your Palm Pilot updated may be the biggest challenge, especially if you've had the luxury of a secretary all these years. Now that you're scheduling your own appointments, you

need to remember the following:

☐ If possible, talk directly to the person you are going to be seeing so you can set the stage for the appointment.

☐ If you can't speak to this person, get to know his or her secretary, who may be the most important person of all. Individuals who set appointments for their managers or employers have control and power because they have access to the person you want to see. Treat them with respect. Ask for their name, and address them by it. Note the name in your records so when you call back you can personalize your call. Develop that relationship.

☐ When making an appointment, be sure you restate the date, time, and place, and put it on your calendar. You don't want to be calling back asking for clarification. It's all right to ask for directions—once! Finally, be certain to reconfirm your appointment the day before your meeting.

What to wear, particularly for men, is becoming more of an issue since the inception of the casual Friday mode. Do you wear a tie or not? My rule of thumb has always been, if unsure, err on the side of being too formal rather than less formal.

Much of this depends on the type of meeting. If it's a formal job interview, more formality will be the rule. For an informational interview, less formality might be right. You don't want to give the impression that you're trying too hard or you're too desperate. Also, you might need to "lighten up" with individuals you know and are seeing just to make connections. If you have recently left a position, people are going to be asking you and others how you are doing and how you are handling things. This is especially true if there are rumors (and there will be) regarding your departure. Impression management is important. You want people to walk away saying that Gary looks great and seems to be really happy, "the best I've seen him look in years."

Having to respond to individuals who think you've lost your job, rather than ever assuming it was your choice, and talk to you as if they are speaking to a victim is to be expected. They may not know exactly what to say, so be upbeat, be confident, and be in control. When they say to you, "What can I say?" you answer, "Say congratulations. This is a good thing for me!" Even if they don't believe you, at the minimum they would have to say that you are handling it well. Again, people will say what they want to, anyway.

Immediately after your appointment or interview, summarize what transpired. Make specific notes on any follow-up resulting from your meeting. Mark in your calendar or Palm Pilot a reminder or confirmation of additional meetings or call-backs.

Send out an immediate thank you and remind that person of any follow-up meeting or task they said they would perform in your behalf. For instance, "It was great meeting with you today, and I truly appreciate your willingness to contact so and so."

Ask Yourself

Activity

The importance of reconnecting with individuals from prior personal and professional experiences cannot be overstated as you begin your job search. You never know what person or what past experience will hold the key to your future employment.

Use the following chart to identify possible sources for networking and reconnection. By "Key Experience," think about that particular project, interaction, or decision that would remind the individual you are calling of you in the most positive light. Wouldn't it be beneficial to be able to start off the conversation with "Remember when we...," or "I often think about the time...." These past recollections can make the difference in re-establishing rapport and credibility.

Networking and Reconnecting Tracking Chart

Work Experiences	Key Experience	Contact	Contact Information
A.			
B.			
C.			
D.			
Volunteer Experiences			
A.			
B.			
C.			
D.			
Professional Organization Experiences			
A.			
B.			
C.			
D.			
Personal Experiences			
A.			
B.			
C.			
D.			

Recommended Resources

Books

The following books represent some of the best resources for organizing and implementing an effective networking campaign:

Foot in the Door, Katharine Hansen (Ten Speed Press, 2000)

Golden Rule of Schmoozing, Aye Jaye (Sourcebooks, 1998)

How to Work a Room, 2nd Edition, Susan RoAne (Warner Books, 2000)

Make Your Contacts Count, Anne Baber and Lynne Waymon (AMACOM, 2001)

Masters of Networking, Ivan R. Misner, Don Morgan, et al. (Bard Press, 2000)

Networking Smart, Wayne E. Baker (McGraw-Hill, 1994)

People Power, Donna Fisher (Bard Press, 1995)

Power Networking, Donna and Sandy Vilas (Bard Press, 2000)

Power to Get In, Michael A. Boylan (St. Martin's Press, 1998)

The Savvy Networker, Ron and Caryl Krannich (Impact Publications, 2001)

The Secrets of Savvy Networking, Susan RoAne (Warner Books, 1993)

Online Networking Opportunities

- Cyberfiber   www.cyberfiber.com

- Google   groups.google.com

- JobBankUSA   jobbankusa.com/usejobs.html

- Topica   topica.com

- Usenet Info Center   metalab.unc.edu/usenet-i/
home.html

Employment Websites With Message Boards

- Monster.com   community.monster.com/boards

- Vault.com   vault.com/community/mb/mb_home.jsp

Websites for Sharpening Networking Skills

- WetFeet   wetfeet.com/advice/networking.asp

- Monster.com   content.monster.com/network

- Quintessential Careers   quintcareers.com/
networking.html

- Riley Guide   www.rileyguide.com/netintv.html

- WinningTheJob   www.winningthejob.com

- SchmoozeMonger   www.schmoozemonger.com

- Susan RoAne   susanroane.com/free.html

- Contacts Count   contactscount.com/articles.html

Online Directories of Professional Associations

- Associations on the Net   ipl.org/ref/AON

- AssociationCentral   associationcentral.com

- American Society
  of Association Executives   www.asaenet.org

- GuideStar   guidestar.org

Women's Online Networking Groups

- Advancing Women   advancingwomen.com

- American Association of
  University Women   aauw.org

- American BusinessWomen's Association abwahq.org

- Business Women's
  Network Interactive   BWNi.com

- Federally Employed Women   few.org

- iVillage   ivillage.com

- Systers   systers.org

- Women.com   women.com
- Women's Wire   womenswire.com

Alumni Groups for Networking

- Alumni.net   alumni.net
- Alumniconnections   bcharrispub.com/isd/alumni
                                 connections.html
- Planet Alumni
                                 planetalumni.com

Online Locators For Re-building Networks

- Anywho   anywho.com
- Classmates   classmates.com
- InfoSpace   infospace.com
- KnowX   knowx.com
- Switchboard   switchboard.com
- The Ultimate White Pages   theultimates.com/white
- Whowhere Lycos   whowhere.lycos.com
- WorldPages   worldpages.com
- Yahoo   people.yahoo.com

Online Military Locators and Buddy Finders

- GI Buddies.com   gibuddies.com
- GI Search.com   gisearch.com
- Military.com   military.com
- Military Connections   militaryconnections.com
- Military USA   militaryusa.com

Job Search Clubs and Support Groups

- 5 O'Clock Clubs   fiveoclockclub.com
- 40-Plus Clubs   40plus.org/chapters
- Chicago Jobs   chicagojobs/org/support.html
- ExecuNet   execunet.com
- Professionals in Transition   jobsearching.org

10

Communicating Your
Strengths in Interviews

*"I'm so sick of being called a nice guy. When people
say that they mean he is weak and can't make the hard
decisions. Is this the way I come across?"*

Analyze Your Audience

Just as the public speaker needs to analyze his/her audience before
giving a speech, the same principle can and should be applied to
the interview situation. Before going on the formal job interview,
you should do as much as possible to collect data about the organization. This will not only help you to answer the interviewer's
questions but assist you in formulating questions to ask the interviewer. Again, remember, the interview is a two-way street and
the directions that are given to both you and the interviewer at its
conclusion will determine whether either one of both of you wish
to proceed.

As part of your analysis, the following questions should be asked:

❏ What is the culture of this organization?

❏ What is its history?

❏ What is its record of success?

❏ What is currently going on in the organization?

❏ Who are the people working there?

❏ Whom does it serve?

Conducting an analysis can make all the difference in your approach to the interview and how effectively you communicate during the interview. Your knowledge of the company will also make a statement about your level of interest in working there.

Examine the company's website, annual reports, and brochures. If you don't have access to a computer at home, go to your local public, community college, or university library to conduct an Internet search on the company. When conducting your search, explore other companies or organizations similar to the one where you're being interviewed. Among these might be governmental agencies, nonprofits, publicly and privately owned companies, and large and small organizations. Investigating them will give you added perspective as well as a context for your professional environment. **Bottom line: collect as much data as you can about the organization before the interview process.** This initial assessment will help you to communicate with authority and give you confidence going into the interview.

Review Interview Etiquette: A Primer

Perhaps more important than anything else, particularly for those who have been in management positions and are reentering the job market, is our **attitude** toward the interview. If we haven't had to look for a job for a long time, or we feel our experience or resume should speak for itself, it is easy to understand that our first reaction might be one of resentment and anger. These feelings are only heightened if we are being interviewed by someone who is considerably our junior in age and experience. Chances are this may be the reality and we better learn to deal with it.

Remember in the interview process you are not the one providing the direction, and if you attempt to take on that role or "cop that attitude" the interview is over and done. What you have to do is leave pride and ego at the door and replace them with a recognition that the employment landscape may have changed dramatically since you last looked for a job. You need to polish your interviewing skills, be open to approaching your job search differently than in the past, and adopt a sense of humility. These just might be the key ingredients for landing the right position.

In addition to resentment and anger, you might be feeling pure and simple nervousness. Some of us have really never had to take an interview. We landed our current position through a key contact, re-organization, or a promotion. The idea of engaging in a formal interview process can be daunting and intimidating, particularly if you have not been in the job market for a long time.

Therefore it is helpful to review the fundamentals of interview etiquette that are relevant to the novice job interviewee, but are also important for renewal purposes for those engaged in reentry.

1. Be On Time

If there is one thing that annoys me it's waiting for people who are late. This is critically important in the interview. **Get there early.** One, it is just plain good manners. Two, it gives you an opportunity to get a feel for the "work environment." If the interview is being held at the organization's headquarters, you'll get an idea of the culture of the organization. **Be observant.** Look at the décor, the magazines in the waiting room, the art, certificates or plaques on the wall, interaction among the employees, and the verbal level of their chatter. The "climate" you sense will begin to tell you whether or not you are a good match for this organization. You'll be able to take advantage of all this information if you arrive early. Caution: you don't want to arrive too early or you will appear over-anxious, but five to ten minutes early can give you time to take in all of these factors as well as appearing professional because you're on time.

2. Dress Appropriately

Again, it is very important that you do your homework. Check out the dress norm for the organization. It may have changed since the last time you sought a job. You don't want to walk in with a three-piece suit if everyone else is tieless in short sleeves. While you may not want to be tieless because you're on an interview, your attire can reflect a more casual presence. The worst that you can do is be so overdressed that you look like you own the company rather than wanting to work there.

The primary rule for dressing appropriately is not calling attention to yourself, but wearing clothes that are appropriate to the environment, the colleagues you'll be working with, and the clientele you will be serving. Even within these boundaries you will still be able to express your individualism. While women have always been comfortable caring about their clothes and being precise about their style of dress, men have typically felt uncomfortable showing the same level of caring and detail. It was not considered macho. That is no longer the case. The way you look, whether you are a man or a woman, can be the deciding factor in getting the job, advancing, or attracting the customer or client. Fortunately or unfortunately, appearances and clothing matter.

If you need help in deciding what is appropriate there are numerous books on the market such as JoAnna Nicholson's *Dressing Smart for Men* and *Dressing Smart for Women* (Impact Publications, 2003) and Susan Bixler's *The New Professional Image* (Adams Media, 1997), which can give you some general guidelines, as well as magazines like *Gentleman's Quarterly*, *Vanity Fair*, or *Vogue*, which can give you a glimpse of the latest styles and fashions. Perusing through magazines that cater to your industry, or trade publications, can give provide a good barometer on what is appropriate in that particular workplace setting. If you look at the ads in that magazine and the photographs of individuals working in the field, you can begin to get a feel for what works and what doesn't.

Also, consider getting help from a professional. In every city where I have lived I have gone to the store in the community that is frequented by my contemporaries and working colleagues and tried to identify a salesperson, hopefully one who has been there a while and is familiar with the merchandise, to guide me in my selections on a continuing basis. This person becomes your professional and personal shopper. I have found this person will look out for me, identifying items that would be appropriate, sometimes putting them on hold or watching them for me so that I have them when they go on sale, and selecting things when I'm out of town and sending them to me. This kind of assistance has saved me time and money over and over again and it doesn't cost anything. Also it is wonderful to walk into a store and have someone greet you and give you the service and respect that you and your position deserve.

3. Break the Ice

If you're offered coffee or a soft drink during the interview, **take it** even if you are not thirsty. It helps to break the ice, gives you a bit more time to study your surroundings, and it also gives you a prop when you're in the midst of the interview. Did you ever notice on the David Letterman and Jay Leno shows that the guests are usually sipping a beverage of some kind. Are they that thirsty? Was it that long a trek from the Green Room to the stage? No, it's a prop. It gives the guests a chance to catch their breath, to be reflective. One piece of advice: If they ask you if you want coffee, don't give 15 directions telling them how you want it. No café latte here. Chances are you won't even drink it all.

4. Close and Take Action?

At the end of the interview, have a clear sense of what comes next. Are they going to call you? Are you going to follow up with them? Are you supposed to get in touch with another party? Is that other person going to be getting in touch with you? **Make sure this is clear**, otherwise you'll be obsessing in the car going home as to your next appointment and what you need to do. **Follow-up** is extremely important, but you don't want to waste a great deal of time figuring out what it is you're supposed to do. Writing summary notes on each encounter will help you to avoid this problem.

While follow-up is important, what you don't want to do is hound the interviewer or employer with frequent calls or notes inquiring on the status of their search process. One, you don't want to appear desperate, and two, it can be extremely annoying. Before the end of the interview, ask the interviewer what their timetable is for filling the position. Also you might say, "If I don't hear from you in the next two weeks, is it all right if I give you a call to check on the status of the position?" More than likely, the interviewer will be comfortable with this, or they will simply say they will contact you. Don't press them. **Follow their instructions.**

5. Follow Up

Immediately after your interview, follow up with a thank you letter. You can never thank people enough for their time or their wisdom and advice. In some instances, a handwritten note will be more appropriate than a form letter. Either way, don't delay. Get it out immediately. Also use the thank you letter to remind them of the next step each of you needs to take in following up with your interview.

Effective Communication: The Basics

One of the first axioms of all communication theory is the principle "You cannot **not** communicate." When I first heard this axiom some 30 years ago in a communications class taught by my professor and mentor, Dr. Raymond Tucker, it seemed so profound. Now, of course, with hundreds of self-help books on the shelves (including this one), CNN, the Internet, and God knows whatever other technological life force is out there, this is even more obvious. However, the principle still holds true. It's just that the conclusion might be made more quickly. We need to remember that everything we do, **everything we say verbally or nonverbally, makes a statement.** In less than ten seconds in any interaction, the other person is already forming impressions and drawing conclusions about you. They have already decided, to some degree, whether they like or dislike you based on that brief span of time. Don't underestimate the importance of **likability.** It is an important dimension in communication and is even more significant when you're taking the job interview.

Effective Communication and Likability Factors

The elements of likability are not rocket science, but common sense and a reflection of what we all find attractive in other people. What makes us remember an individual beyond that brief encounter? What makes us feel positive about that person? What makes us want to see that person again? Regardless of whether it's an interview or just a social event, the following elements can make a difference in communicating effectively and raising your level of "likability."

1. Be Positive

Project a positive image or aura. People who are positive give us energy. They invigorate and inspire us.

They bring out the best in us. Likewise, people who are negative sap our energy and take the life-blood out of us. **Projecting a positive image is not only reflected in the spoken language we use but the nonverbal cues we exhibit.** In fact, many would say that nonverbal communication is much more critical in projecting what we are feeling than any words we use. Direct eye contact, a firm handshake, a lilt in your voice, good posture, an overall air of confidence and pride in yourself are more important than any words you might say. Remember, since impressions are made in a matter of seconds, use them wisely and make sure that the meta-communication—the communication about your communication—is consistent. For example, if you're trying to convey a feeling of confidence but your shoulders are slouched and you're not looking the person in the eye, you're giving mixed signals, and chances are that individual will draw conclusions about you from what you **didn't** say.

2. Be Spontaneous

In an age where technology seems to be the rule of the day and a robotic response on a voice message is certainly not uncommon, it is not the image we want to project in our own communication. Although some of us are more spontaneous than others, each of us needs to maximize our willingness to be spontaneous. This is particularly true in a job interview that is inherently a stilted encounter. Your fresh and creative side needs to be projected. **Let the interviewer know a little bit more about you than your resume might reveal.** What do you do to have fun? What are your hobbies? What were your proudest moments? Your answers to these questions can be more revealing than anything else you say.

For example, I recently heard of someone who was interviewing for a job with a rather conservative accounting firm. It was clear the competition was stiff, and there being a number of qualified candidates. While this person certainly had the qualifications and the experience, he knew that this was true of many of the other candidates. What would set him apart from the rest? During the interview, the interviewer asked him what he did in his spare time. He mentioned among other things that he had done some community theater, not the typical response you would expect to hear from an accountant.

As it turns out the interviewer was on the board of the local community theater, and as a result conversation ensued about the business side of theater and the arts. The interview no longer was an interview but a conversation, and the rapport between the interviewer and the interviewee intensified. By the way, he got the job. Who would have predicted that his interest in something totally outside the job description would clinch it for him? Granted, he had all the other chits but so did many others applying for the position. This spontaneous conversation and his willingness to share another side of himself made it happen.

3. Be Honest

While "spin" and packaging of yourself have their place and are expected, particularly in the job interview, it is more important that spin and packaging never sacrifice honesty and a true representation of who you are. **You need to project your values and principles and not alter or prostitute them to get the job or make the deal.** While you might solve that problem or land that job in the short term, you will be conflicted with this down the road. The same is true regarding your abilities and talents. In our attempt to sell ourselves, all of us might embellish, but the worst thing you can do is to create false expectations, or expectations that can't be reached but will only cause unnecessary pressure once you have gotten what you think you want. The old cliché "Be careful, you might get what you wished for" is particularly cautionary if achieved through dishonest communication.

The question of how honest you should be regarding why you left your last position can be especially tricky, particularly if the language of your separation agreement, if you even had one, states that you may not discuss the details. In these instances, you will need to be true to the document you signed and attempt to deflect the question. However, in general, it pays to be honest. There is no question that the truth will come out anyway. Better you should tell your version of your departure than someone else. The worst scenario would be for you to paint one picture only to have it invalidated through reference checks or further investigation. Using phrases like "It was mutual," "It was time for both myself and the organization," or "I read the tea leaves" may sometimes be adequate responses to these sensitive questions, but in some instances you will be asked to be more specific. If you are, answering the question as it relates to changing job demands might help, particularly if the job you are applying for necessitates skills that are your strengths. For instance the following sample conversation might be helpful:

Interviewer: So if you were as successful as you say you were, why did you leave your position?

Interviewee: When I was hired for the position, the main task was to put the organization back on track, create a new team, increase morale, and then focus on the big picture. I did that and I did that well. I found myself more and more having to deal with the administrative details of the organization. This is not what I want to be doing nor is it my strength. It was time for me to go. I knew it and the organization knew it.

One other point: In increasingly political environments, especially in top CEO positions, "getting fired" or leaving a position is more acceptable today than it used to be, particularly if the reason the person left was due to a difference in philosophy or agreeing to disagree on key issues. This may even be interpreted as having strong convictions or taking risk, both valuable commodities.

4. Be Clear and Concise

In communicating, skip the nonsense and **try to be as precise and concise as possible in answering questions and inquiries**. "Cut to the chase" as they say in responding to the probe of the interviewer. However, this does not mean that you respond to questions with yes or no answers. Sometimes responding with "The short answer to your question is 'yes', but allow me to elaborate" can be the best response. Your immediate yes or no answer will let the interviewer know you are not avoiding the question or hedging, but also give you an opportunity to provide more detail.

5. Be Passionate

"What the world needs now is passion." If there is one thing that sets one person apart from another it is passion. **There is no substitute for people who express enthusiasm and passion** for what they do and excitement when they talk about their interests and what they would bring to any position. Very often, it is the "P" factor that will separate you from everyone else. While content and knowledge are critical factors among equally qualified candidates, the "P" factor may get you the job. However, be careful. You don't want to come across as a "cheerleader" expressing emotion and no substance. Demonstrate your passion through example and conviction for what you do.

6. Be an Active Listener

Have you ever been with someone who never seems to listen to you but is only interested in what their own response might be? Have you ever been with someone who responds before you do, finishes your sentences, interrupts while you're speaking? This is a very self-centered individual. The opposite of this is someone who listens with empathy, with understanding, with interest.

In the interview situation, you want to be an active listener. Don't be concerned with getting all of your points covered. **If you listen to the interviewer, what you need to say will be said.**

In the best of worlds, the interviewer will give you the opportunity to do the talking and not monopolize the situation. Unfortunately, this is not always the case. Because of ego, power, or position, the interviewer may use this opportunity for personal ego gratification rather than finding out about you. The worst thing you can do is try to play this game. You won't win. Instead, react as much as possible to the comments and try to get your points covered. You may decide after this encounter that you could never work for this person, but at least he will walk away with a good impression of you. Remember, the interview operates under the Rule of Reciprocity—both the interviewer and interviewee have something to offer and exchange. Just as she has the opportunity to offer a position, you have the opportunity to refuse it.

Ask Yourself

Activity A

Impressions are made almost immediately, and the way you dress for the job interview is extremely important, since it not only makes a statement about you but gives an indication of whether or not you would be the right "fit" for the organization. As already stated, not every job interview requires the same kind of dress. Some organizations or businesses are more formal than others, and your presentation should reflect the culture of the organization. Doing your homework about the organization ahead of time will provide you with the information you need to determine what you will wear.

Take stock of your wardrobe. Do you have the basic tools for the job interview? Is it versatile enough to match the organization with a more "formal culture" or one that is more informal.

Once you have done that, go to the local bookstore or newsstand and browse through the pages of professionally based magazines that cater to your kind of industry and get a sense from the photographs what successful people in the industry are wearing and what the culture of that industry or field reflects. Remember, look at the pictures of the winners.

Activity B

The concept of "audience analysis" is extremely important in the job interview. If you haven't analyzed the audience—in this case the interviewer and the organization the interviewer represents—you are not going to be successful in communicating effectively.

Check out the websites of two potential employers. Take, for example, The Boston Consulting Group: www.bcg.com. What kind of image do they project? What conclusions can you draw from these images? How would your approach in applying to these organizations differ in light of the information you've ascertained?

Activity C

Likability is not only a key ingredient in all interpersonal relationships but is particularly critical in the job interview. Employers, as we know, will very often make their final decision on the basis of subjective factors rather than on objective ones, particularly if two potential candidates are equal on those objective criteria. What makes likability even more complex in the job interview is that impressions are made in a very short period of time.

With that in mind, reflect on five individuals whom you consider to be extremely likable and five individuals whom you rate low on the likability scale. What behaviors do the two groups of individuals project? Are the likability factors similar in the five individuals? Are those traits that alienate similar? What kinds of behaviors do you project? Can you integrate some of the likability traits into your own personality? Can you develop them so they can work to your advantage in the job interview?

Recommended Resources

Books

101 Dynamite Answers to Interview Questions, Caryl and Ron Krannich (Impact Publications, 2000)

101 Dynamite Questions to Ask at Your Job Interview, Richard Fein (Impact Publications, 2001)

101 Great Answers to the Toughest Interview Questions, 4th *Edition,* Ron Fry (Career Press, 2000)

250 Job Interview Questions You'll Most Likely Be Asked, Peter Veruki (Adams Media, 1999)

Haldane's Best Answers to Tough Interview Questions, Bernard Haldane Associates (Impact Publications, 2000)

Interview for Success, 8th Edition, Caryl and Ron Krannich (Impact Publications, 2003)

Interview Rehearsal Book, Deb Gottesman and Buzz Mauro (Berkley Publishing Group, 1999)

Job Interviews for Dummies, 2nd Edition, Joyce Lain Kennedy (John Wiley & Sons, 2000)

Naked at the Interview, Burton Jay Nadler (John Wiley & Sons, 1994)

The Perfect Interview, 2nd Edition, John Drake (AMACOM, 1997)

Power Interviews, Revised Edition, Neil M. Yeager and Lee Hough (John Wiley & Sons, 1998)

Savvy Interviewing, Caryl and Ron Krannich (Impact Publications, 2000)

Sweaty Palms, H. Anthony Medley (Ten Speed Press, 1992)

Winning Interviews for $100,000+ Jobs, Wendy S. Enelow (Impact Publications, 1999)

Websites

- Monster.com   interview.monster.com
  content.monster.com/jobinfo/interview

- JobInterview.net   job-interview.net

- Interview Coach   interviewcoach.com

- Quintessential Careers   quintcareers.com/intvres.html

- Riley Guide   rileyguide.com/netintv.html

- WinningTheJob   winningthejob.com

11

Coping With Your
Mood Swings

*"I feel very anxious this morning. One insecurity
seems to lead to another."*

It **is very important** that during the course of your job
search or career change you keep reminding yourself of
your accomplishments and those instances in your life
where you were most proud of yourself. Instances where perhaps
you had taken an initiative or did something surprising and spontaneous that resulted in something that you didn't expect. Each of
us has our own stories of these small victories, some that we even
remember from childhood, and recalling them can help ease the
pain and give us strength.

During my own job search, I kept thinking about the time
when I was 12 years old and desperately wanted a new wrist
watch, which my parents could not afford to buy me. It just so
happened that one afternoon my uncle, in a conversation with my
mother, mentioned that a friend of his had become a watch tester
for the Timex Corporation. (Remember John Cameron Swayzee?)
My ears perked up upon overhearing this. I immediately began
drafting a letter to Timex telling them my situation in the most
dramatic terms I could muster and requesting to be a tester.

While I did not receive much encouragement from my mother, I would still go to the mailbox everyday expecting a package from Timex. Lo and behold, six weeks later I received a letter from Timex informing me that I was now an official Timex tester. My first test watch was already in the mail. From that day forward for ten years I would test Timex watches, wearing them, monitoring their accuracy, and returning them if they didn't come up to speed, only to receive a new one and begin the process again.

What this childhood memory points out for me (if only I had reminded myself of it more often) is the importance of taking a chance, picking up on an opportunity, and acting on an instinct or a feeling that may or may not yield any results. In most instances what do you have to lose? Even when those around you are saying it's not worth it or it's not going to work, weigh the risks and take a shot. Sending that letter or that resume, or making that phone call for a position that may seem out of reach just might be the one that can lead you in a direction you never knew even existed.

At the same time I don't want to exaggerate the importance of this story, nor understate the fact that the process of looking for a job or changing careers can be a very stressful and anxiety-producing experience even under the best of circumstances. That's the reality, and you will need to accept it.

You might find yourself in a very manic state of mind. One day you'll feel fine, even high with the thought of all the possibilities that await you, while other days you will feel defeated, unproductive, and panic that you'll never get another job or career opportunity. You'll begin to question your worth, your skills, and whether or not you can compete with a new reality and a younger generation of job seekers. This is natural, yet at the same time it can become demoralizing. You might be, moving from a state of idealism to frustration to demoralization. If that's where you find yourself at this moment, the following **coping skills** will be useful:

Develop a List of "Positive Counselors"

In your corner are going to be some individuals who can always be depended on to pull you up and bolster your sagging ego. Call upon these individuals for **advice** and **reassurance**. Use them to remind you of your strengths, your value, and your self-worth. These people might be past colleagues, friends, or passing associates, but they will help you get through the difficult days. One note of caution: don't exhaust any one of them, for even the best of friends don't necessarily want the role of therapist. Also, don't depend on your spouse to always be this person, as they are dealing with their own insecurities and anxieties regarding the future.

Stick to Your Schedule and Your Daily Structure

A sense of order and a daily routine will not only keep you **focused** but also **anchored**. It will take your mind off the long term by focusing on what needs to be done now. There will be the temptation to only complete the easy tasks or the more passive tasks like writing a letter or sending out a resume. The task of making calls to set up appointments or to contact people you haven't seen in may years but who could help you now will be more difficult. Yet if you have scheduled the difficult as well as the easy tasks on your calendar, the more likely you are to complete them. In developing your daily calendar, group these tasks into specific hourly time frames so that you have a definite beginning and end for their completion. Make sure you put those you haven't completed today on tomorrow's schedule.

Don't Stay in the Office All Day

The last thing you want to do is stay in your "home office" all day. The more you **interact with people** on a social or professional level the more opportunity there will be to make the right connection. Make a luncheon appointment. Go to the gym. Go to a bookstore and look at the latest self-help book. Do something to get yourself out of your office. Try to integrate into each day something that gives you joy, makes you laugh, renews your spirits, and moves you one step further in achieving your professional goal.

Develop the Next Day's Strategy

It's very important to have a sense of direction for the following day, just as you did when you were working. Develop some **goals**, even simple ones. Knowing that you have some very specific activities you can carry out the following day will give you comfort and momentum.

Try a Little Reinvention

Another way of coping with the whole process of change is considering the notion of personal reinvention. If this is a time for new beginnings, is this also a time for a "**new you**"? Is this the time to begin a new diet, change the color of your hair or the approach to your wardrobe? While these changes may seem frivolous or shallow, they can often have a direct impact on your self-image and how you interact with other people. We all know that when we feel good about ourselves, we develop a sense of liberation. We often take more risks and have a generally more positive outlook on the world. While individuals who know you may be shocked or even resistant to the "new you," others will be seeing you for the first time and defining you from that first impression. Take advantage of your newfound freedom before you have to begin the formal interview process, and give yourself the luxury of a little reinvention before you go public.

Go to Sleep Feeling Good

End every day feeling positive. The old expression "Don't go to bed angry" can be extrapolated to your current situation: don't go to sleep without feeling good. In order to ensure this, do something **positive**. Call one of your positive counselors; go out to dinner with your wife; go to the movies with your son or daughter. Try to conclude each day on a positive note. That will not only ensure a better night's sleep, but will start your new day with renewed energy.

Ask Yourself

Activity

Sticking to a **daily schedule** and structure is extremely important while you are in the process of your job and career exploration, particularly if you are based at home. It will be very easy to waste time and seduce yourself into thinking that you can always begin tomorrow.

Develop a daily schedule which incorporates the following elements:

- Phone time for

  - appointment making
  - reconnecting
  - conversations with "positive counselors"

- Mailings –sending out resumes, letters

- Research—the Internet, library, career centers at neighboring colleges and universities, local and regional newspapers, trade journals, employment agencies, and job fairs being held in the area

- Breakfast, lunch, and dinner meetings –informational interviews, reconnecting, networking

- Creative time—writing, research, resume development

- Personal time—exercise, pursuing a hobby, family, friends

12

Are There Other Options?

" Why didn't I listen to my father? Be your own boss,
he would say over and over again."

If you are a **Baby Boomer** like me, when many of you were growing up, the question "What do you want to be?" was much easier to answer and much more definitive. You were either going to be a doctor, a lawyer, a teacher, a nurse, or an engineer. In fact, there was the expectation that you would have the answer to that question very early in life. The pressure to commit yourself to a major in college was intense, for you typically had to declare it in your junior year. Once you completed your education, it was assumed that you would continue to be the doctor, the attorney, the teacher, or the nurse for the rest of your life. You were locked in until you got the gold watch. Likewise, if you went to work for a particular company, it was expected that you would stay with that company for your entire career. Today, we know that is not true. Individuals change and start careers at later stages of their life. In addition, people create new careers and new opportunities for themselves as a result of their life experiences.

Does It Have to Be One Job?

Have you ever considered **melding together** all that you know and all of your experience and do a number of things at the same time, whether it is a combination of consulting, teaching, writing, etc.? Can you craft an acceptable income and lifestyle for yourself in a nontraditional manner and not focus on one set career but a constellation of things within a given framework? Perhaps this range of activities qualifies you to be a consultant in a particular area. While I am not going to address the specifics of starting a consulting business, I want to point out that if you are considering this option, you must factor in financial requirements, time constraints, tolerance for ambiguity and uncertainty, particularly in lean times, and finally, your ability to continuously market yourself. When assessing a steady job versus the possibility of consulting or starting your own business, it also becomes a question of time. Don't fool yourself into thinking that being in your own business takes less time. That is not the case. In addition to the time spent on the services you're offering, you'll be spending time marketing yourself and manning the business side of your new venture.

Yet, regardless of what you decide to do, allow yourself the opportunity to entertain such thoughts. The bottom line is you have to look at all possibilities simultaneously. While you're going about making the calls, sending out the letters, going for the interviews, affiliating with the search firms, you need to also explore the more creative possibilities. Again, this may be the one time in your life that you have the luxury of looking "out of the box," or acting on a professional fantasy that you have had for a long time. You need to ask yourself, "How can I parlay my life experience and my professional achievements into a career?" You may find this is not as difficult as it seems. Finally, **if you don't do it now, then when**?

This question is particularly pertinent if you are over 50 and you're thinking of taking a position rather than striking out on your own. If you take "the position" rather than doing something independently, you run the risk of having, in most instances, to abandon your dream of independence as you settle for a steady job. If you should lose this job or find that it's just not working, and you want to go back to the idea of being your own boss, you've lost that much more time and start-up energy. Again, there is always the possibility of having both, but that, too, has its inherent problems. These are hard decisions and must be thoroughly thought out in consultation with others.

Discuss these options with your positive counselors as well as those individuals whom you have identified as successful, along with the realists who can make you face the realities of your options. Again, don't try to handle everything yourself. **Share the burden** judiciously with selected others. This is not a game. This is not a macho or feminist test. **This is your life**, and you want the best advice you can receive from yourself and others.

Location, Location, Location

How wedded are you geographically? Have you ever contemplated moving? Maybe this is the time to consider a change in venue that you've thought about numerous times before. At the minimum, explore the possibilities of this. The obvious first step in the process is to identify your geographical preferences. You probably already know them. Do you have any contacts there? Is this an opportunity to get in touch with those contacts and go out and visit? Can you arrange for a few informational interviews that will give you a sense of the possibilities?

If you do decide to consider relocating, are you taking into consideration the obvious factors such as cost of living, state income tax (a shocker if you haven't been paying it), schools and education, and general living expenses? Another issue to consider is how soon you could move? Would you want your family to be able to move at the same time? Would you be willing to commute for a temporary period of time or permanently? What are the cost factors in maintaining two residences?

As I mentioned previously, the issue of moving was something I had to confront. With an eleventh grade daughter, I was not about to take her our of school in her junior year even though she'd have her bags packed if we were relocating to either New York or California. My wife and I discussed the reality, and I decided that, if necessary, I would commute for her two remaining high school years. This, of course, becomes a very personal decision totally contingent on your circumstances, but is a scenario you need to examine. As difficult as it may be, you should look at the long-term potential of any position while you are dealing with the short-term realities now.

Ask Yourself

Activity

While you're searching for the "ideal job" you may also want to consider other possibilities such as starting your own business or pursuing a combination of work experiences at the same time. Is it possible to turn a hobby or an avocation into a full-time job?

Here is an opportunity to dream a little. If you could spend your time doing anything at all, what would it be? How could you go about making it happen? How can you parlay your life experience or avocation into a profession or business? Can you identify individuals in your own community who have done this? Set up five informational interviews, conversations designed to give you information and perspective, with these individuals focusing on the following questions:

❑ What was the most difficult aspect of transitioning from your career to what you are doing now?

❑ What was the most surprising discovery in making your dream a reality?

❑ What personal characteristics did you find most helpful in achieving your goal?

❑ What personal characteristics created the most difficulties?

❑ How long did it take you to get from the
dream to the reality?

❑ Was it worth it?

❑ If you have any advice to give, what would
it be?

13

Narrowing Down To
A Final Decison

*"I feel like I'm on a roller coaster. Part of it is I really
don't know what I want to do."*

By **this time,** your search for the "perfect job" has
taken shape. You've identified preferable work
environments and job directions. You've learned
that the sooner you honed in on these two elements, the easier
the job exploration process became. You may have also realized
the job-seeking process is easier for the individual who has one
outstanding skill, because that person knows exactly where to
look and how to respond to if someone asks, "What do you want
to do?" This can also be a limitation, particularly if there is a glut
of people in that particular field, but possessing a dominating
skill does provide focus. On the other hand, people who are
"generalists," who can do many things in a variety of environments, might find the narrowing down process difficult, and the
articulation of what they want to do elusive.

In narrowing down possible work environments and career
directions, you've also identified those individuals and resources
that will be most helpful to you. For instance, you may have found
that two particular search firms are the most productive for you,

two different Internet websites have the more pertinent listings, and five contact people provide the most leads. While you still need to continue seeing as many people as possible and exploring other Internet and search firms' possibilities, use your time wisely. Every possibility is not always an opportunity, and you don't want to fill your day with activities that aren't going to lead you anywhere. Satisfying your need to say to yourself and others that you're seeing lots of people may not result in any payoff. A **more focused approach** at this point rather than a helter-skelter approach is preferable.

Ultimately, offers will come forward. You'll also know what is going to materialize and what won't. Depending on your circumstances, there will be a great **temptation** to take the first substantial offer that comes your way. You'll think of the security, the anxiety about your family, and the discomfort of not being able to answer the question of "What do you do?" in social encounters. You'll be tempted to accept that first "real" offer, but resist the temptation because very often your decision will be based on practical issues and not on job fulfillment and quality of life issues. While an offer may provide you financial security, it may also offer you all the insecurity, unhappiness, and stress you had before. Only this time, it may be much more difficult to start all over. **This decision is an extremely important one and you must truly weigh all the factors.**

Call it cognitive dissonance, call it self-doubt, regardless of what you call it, chances are whatever final career decision you make you will find yourself going back and forth on the wisdom of your decision. The best thing you can do is to **give it your own personal test.** Does the "new job" or career meet the criteria you have already established in your mind? Chances are, it won't meet all the standards, but it needs to meet some critical ones:

1. Financial Needs

It always comes back to dollars, doesn't it? It is not only important that the compensation for your new position meets your financial needs but also meets your psychological and ego needs.

- ☐ If you would be earning less than you were making before, how will you feel?

- ☐ Will the salary necessitate taking on extra work or another job on the side and spreading yourself too thin?

- ☐ Will your new employer even allow you to moonlight?

- ☐ Are you programming yourself for failure and are you setting yourself up for added anxiety and stress that may be worse than what you experienced previously?

In addition to salary, what are the other benefits? Health care coverage, pension plan, sick days, vacation time, all of these factors need to be considered as you negotiate your compensation package.

Make sure you ask these questions **now**. Don't get so caught up in the celebration of getting and accepting an offer without knowing the total package. If possible, set all of these items in writing. Make sure they meet the criteria of your personal "business plan" and that you don't accept a position that does not meet your personal and financial needs.

The answers to these questions become moot if you have no choice but to take the position. Chances are, however, if you have done what I have suggested up until now, you'll have the luxury of choice, a choice that not only meets your financial needs but also your psychic and quality of life needs.

2. Psychic Needs

What do I mean by psychic needs? Is this some New Age mumbo jumbo that seems to resonate in an era of re-awakening spirituality? No, what I'm talking about here are questions related to the (A) work environment and culture of the organization, (B) sense of teamwork and collaboration, and (C) mission of the organization.

Let's start with the last one of these factors first—**mission of the organization**. This relates to your motivation for taking the position. Are you taking it because you believe in the product or mission of the organization, or, at this point in your life, is your primary motivation the money?

When I told a friend about my own career choices, he said, "You've always done something of substance, something that has made a difference in someone's life or the community in general." If that describes you, how comfortable will you be in a professional situation where for the most part the end result is making money? How important is that? How important is feeling passionate about what you're doing? In the long run, will the lack of passion affect your productivity and ultimately impact on your success?

If you speak to many people who are in the midst of mid-career changes, they will often tell you that they are now looking for a position that gives them a feeling of accomplishment, personal satisfaction, and a knowledge that they are making a difference. Are you one of those individuals? Can you have all of these in the position you are considering accepting? They may not be mutually exclusive, but they need to be considered.

Another factor in your psychic needs is your sense of **team and collaboration:**

- ❒ Do you like working alone or prefer to feel part of a group or something larger than yourself?

- ❒ Do your creative and entrepreneurial juices operate independently or through interacting with a team of individuals, colleagues, or partners in a collective endeavor?

- ❒ Are you going to be entering an environment that allows for individual growth, but also encourages collaboration and partnership?

The answer to these questions may determine whether the career option and the organization you are considering are really the right fit.

The last factor is the **culture of the organization** you are considering.

- ❏ What is the culture of this organization?

- ❏ What is the morale of its employees?

- ❏ What kinds of feelings do you get when you walk into the building or suite of offices?

- ❏ Does it seem relaxed or does it seem tense?

- ❏ Is the setting professional enough for you or is it too laid back? Does the organizational environment match your personal style and way of thinking?

- ❏ Would you be proud saying you were part of this organization?

There are no right or wrong answers to any of these questions. It is simply a matter of compatibility between you and the organization.

The test of compatibility with the organizational culture is extremely important, for while you may have the technical skills to do the job, the chemistry between yourself and the environment can be the critical factor in your job satisfaction. The best way to get a gauge of the organizational culture is through observation. Perhaps before you accept the offer you can arrange to observe the environment for a day or two. This may not be something the organization will suggest, so you may have to suggest it to them. They will accommodate your request if they want you badly enough. Remember, both you and the organization are making an investment in your success so it pays to make sure the decision is the right one. Also, informal conversations with employees can help you determine the cultural temperature of the organization and assist you in determining if this is going to work.

Another element of organizational culture can be measured by the loyalty and longevity of the employees:

- ❒ How long have your potential co-workers been working there? What is the turnover rate?

- ❒ Have people been promoted from within?

- ❒ What opportunities are there for individual creativity and self-expression?

While you will not be able to anticipate every question to ask ahead of time, answers to questions relating to mission, collegial relations, and organizational culture will probably be better predictions of job fulfillment than any other factors including financial ones.

Ask Yourself

Activity

Chances are your acceptance or rejection of a job offer will not be based on a single factor but a combination of factors. Reflecting on the dimensions outlined in this chapter, assess the wisdom of accepting any job offer by checking those items that are most important to you. Does the job offer these? Do you have other personal requirements that are not included here? In identifying those elements that are most important to you here, you can then use your list to evaluate any offers that come your way. In doing this you will develop a minimum set of criteria for evaluating any job opportunity.

1. Financial Considerations:

☐ Salary

☐ Benefits (e.g., sick days, vacation, health insurance)

☐ Pension

☐ Financial incentives (e.g., stock options, commissions, bonuses)

☐ Raises/salary increases

2. Psychic Considerations:

☐ Mission of the organization

❐ Work environment or culture

❐ Work space and office aesthetics

❐ Working relationships (feelings about co-workers)

❐ Constituent or client-based relationships (feelings about those you're serving)

❐ Work ethic

❐ Organizational value system

14

Checklist Of Survival Tips

*"Regardless of what we think of Madonna or Bill
Clinton, they have been masters of re-inventing
themselves and in the process, have
re-energized their careers."*

As **I mentioned** in Chapter 11, "Coping With
Your Mood Swings," everyone has their own way
of surviving the transition process, and the career
exploration that follows. The following elements were essential
in keeping me more focused, centered, and sane during my own
personal journey.

Write It Down

Keeping a **daily diary** that ultimately led to the writing of this
book was probably the most significant and helpful tool for me
during this entire process. Writing daily not only helped me bring
routine and structure to my day, but allowed me the vehicle to
express my feelings, try things out, and as a result, gave me confidence in my own thought process.

Daily Routine

Feelings of uselessness, laziness, and guilt will be common as you go through this process. When you've spent your life involved in frenetic activity and being constantly on the go, a sudden halt in this kind of lifestyle, while probably a good thing, can make you question your worth and your utility. Having a **set routine and structure** will not only give you needed order, but direction and purpose. Making finding a job a job will help you make the transition.

Your Computer

Being one of the technologically challenged, I never though I'd be espousing the benefits of interacting with my computer. However, checking career websites on a daily basis and reviewing e-mails give you **a connection not only to individuals but also to the rest of the world.** Now that you've moved from a highly interactive existence to one more defined by isolation and independence, the computer can be very important in making that transition.

Positive Counselors

As I've alluded to a number of times in this book, the debilitating impact of being around negative people cannot be overstated. They will only increase your self-doubt and insecurity rather than provide you with hope and inspiration. The kinds of individuals I'm referring to are different than the "realists" referred to in Chapter 9, who will very often "bring you back down to earth" when your idealism might be taking over your sense of reality. The persons I'm commenting on here are those who only see "the glass half empty" rather than "half full." You cannot afford to be around these people. They will never provide you with the care and feeding your ego needs at this particular point in your life.

Therefore you must tap into that handful of people—and it will only be a handful—who truly support you, can be counted on for ideas, and, most importantly, can be depended on for **their enthusiasm and absolute confidence in you** and your future. They are a life force that you will need to tap over and over again.

Financial Analysis

A **clear understanding** of your financial situation and knowing how long you can "wait it out" will give you the comfort level you need to maintain your excitement about new possibilities. It will also give you the freedom to explore new directions and decrease the overall level of anxiety that comes with any major life change.

Permission to Feel Anxious

The recognition that you will have mood swings and that your level of anxiety will ebb and flow will help you deal with those days where you feel particularly down. **Allow yourself to have these feelings**. They are normal and part of the transition process.

Self-Talk

I used to think that the idea of having a mantra and repeating it to yourself was pure nonsense and was just another by-product of New Age philosophy. I've since learned otherwise. Talking to yourself can be extremely helpful. Just as we have the power to persuade others, we have the power to convince ourselves. We don't want to engage in self delusion but we do want to remind ourselves of our value and our past achievements and accomplishments.

It is clear that it is extremely disconcerting to believe something privately and have to publicly state the opposite. In your job and career exploration, you will constantly be put in the position of having to tout your value and your expertise, so you better believe what you're saying. If you don't express confidence and bravado (yes, bravado), your need to convince others that you are the one for the position will not come through. So, talk to yourself. **Bombard yourself with positive thoughts**. Say it out loud. Very often the best place to engage in this type of self-therapy is in your car. With cell phones and hands-free devices no one will ever know that you are talking to yourself.

A Supportive Spouse or Significant Others

Having a spouse or significant other who is supportive and has ownership in the process you're going through is vital. **You cannot go through this alone.** As mentioned earlier, keeping those who are most important to you in the loop and informed of your progress will give you personal strength as well as reinforcing those relationships.

Know Your Special Power

In Chapter 2, I referred to the special and unique power each of us possess due to certain talents, abilities, or instincts. We need to **remind ourselves of these special gifts** and reflect on how they have helped us succeed and achieve. At this juncture, we can use this power to move in a new career or life direction that can bring us joy and fulfillment. Reminding ourselves of this and seeing the application of our special gifts will continue to give us confidence and added empowerment.

Re-invent Yourself

Using this period of my life to engage in some re-invention was also freeing. In the process, I joined a health club, lost 15 pounds, and my wife says I even grew hair. Each of us does this in our own way. Yet, whether it's a diet, an exercise program, a change in hair color, developing a hobby, or cultivating new relationships, **re-inventing ourselves can help us put our past behind us and move forward.**

Have a Plan

I think all of us would acknowledge that even the most successful people, however we define success, have insecurities and self-doubt. Yet, the difference between these individuals and the rest of us is that they seem to respond to things differently. Why is that? Part of it is the fact that they **have a plan, a set of goals that they wish to achieve, and a timetable for achieving them.** All of us need such a plan for achieving personal and professional aspirations. The development of my own plan provided a map for directing me toward the future.

Timing

Timing may not be everything, but it is a critical factor in new endings and new beginnings. Imagine, if you will, a three-dimensional clock. One side reflects your **psychological timing,** side two reflects your **financial timing,** and the third side reflects the **organizational timing.** By your psychological timing I am referring to your ability to read the signs discussed in Chapter 2 and reaching the conclusion that you have to start anew and begin that process now. Your financial timing is assessing the financial factors which will determine the possibilities of your exit from one situation and entrance into another, and the organizational timing refers to those environmental factors that allow you to move forward now. An accurate reading of these three sides of the clock for determining your next step must be analyzed with care if you are to move on with your personal and professional life with order rather than chaos. Being aware of my personal timetable and setting specific deadlines for completing each task propelled me to the next one without turning into the "Mad Hatter."

15

It's A New Beginning

"It's amazing how I've worked in a field for practically 15 years, and I truly don't feel a sense of loss. I always felt there was another career out there."

The **final chapter** of this book will be different for every individual who is reading it, since each of us is a product of our own personal experience and will ultimately make our own decisions regarding our professional future. I hope this book has addressed some of your professional needs and answered some questions, but has also helped you reflect on your feelings and given you strategies for making some personal and professional changes. For me, writing this book has been cathartic in many ways. In fact, as I've noted before, I would recommend the process of writing to each of you, for everyone has a story to tell, lessons to give and experience to share.

One such person who had a great deal to share was my friend Sadie. My wife and I "adopted" Sadie when she was 92. She was a feisty little woman who while in her nineties still lived in a second story walk-up. Sadie had a daily routine. She would go to the Golden Age Club everyday at the local community center and on weekends would attend religious services on both Friday and

Saturdays. That's where we met Sadie one day when she needed a ride home and had asked us if we were going in her direction. From that point on for the next 14 years, Sadie became part of our lives and taught us life lessons that I've often reflected on as I've made my way through this journey. I've come to refer to these lessons as Sadie's Rules.

Sadie's Rules

I. Know What You Want

At 72 Sadie was left a widow. While she mourned for her first husband, she realized that in order for her to continue living the life she wanted she would need to remarry. In a short time she met an Englishman who would become her second husband. While Sadie was reluctant to marry and he was not her ideal catch, she knew that with the Englishman came financial security. So with her usual tenacity and resolve Sadie set out to marry him and succeeded. They had been married for ten years when her Englishman died. She was left a widow again, but a more financially secure one, so she would tell it (he left her $10,000). **Sadie had sized up her situation, had set a goal, and had met it.**

2. Look at the Glass Half Full

If you ever asked Sadie if she was happy, she would automatically say, "My gosh, yes! I've been to Hawaii twice, went to Grossingers, had two children, two husbands, and a career [she worked as a saleswoman in a ladies' shop]. All of that and not a high school education." Sadie had her ups and downs in life, but **in her mind she had exceeded her expectations and had done all the things she wanted to do.** She would die a happy woman.

3. It's All Perspective

If you asked Sadie what she had for dinner last night she would say, "Seafood." Well, how did you do that? "Bumblebee." What are you having tonight, Sadie? "Italian." Oh, really, are you going out to an Italian restaurant? "No, just me and Chef Boyardee." And tomorrow? "Oh, I'm having southern, fried chicken and mashed potatoes. I always try to eat southern (Swanson frozen TV dinner] at least once a week." **Sadie could put a spin on almost anything and get you to believe you were missing something.**

4. Life Is a Game

One of Sadie's favorite activities was going to the department store cosmetics counter with my wife. Boy, would they have a good time. Her favorite part of these trips would be to ask the salesperson to guess her age. "How old do you think I am?" she would ask with great pride. They would respond, 75, 85, 90? Of course, Sadie was now approaching 101 and relished telling the salesperson her real age, for, after she did, salespeople from all over the store would run to the counter to talk to her and want to give her samples of all their products. Walking out with a shopping bag of these, Sadie and my wife would race to the car to divide up the booty. **Sadie had learned that life can be joyous if we don't take ourselves too seriously.**

5. Cop Some Attitude

Sadie was known for her many outfits. Everyday she would arrive at the Golden Age Club in a new fashion statement, all of them courtesy of discount stores and flea markets that she would frequent with my wife in hand. Sadie's idea was that at her age quality wasn't as important as the way you carried yourself in whatever you're wearing. She would always say, "I can wear a twenty-dollar hand-me-down and look like a million bucks, while so and so can spend four times as much and look like twenty dollars." Besides, she'd add, "Nothing lasts forever." **Sadie knew that attitude was a critical factor in the way others view you.**

When Sadie was 104 her faculties were still sharp but her body was ready to go and so was she. And knowing her, it was clearly her decision.

Empower Yourself

I learned a great deal from Sadie and I keep her "Rules" in mind as I continue to engage in a sometimes painful but necessary re-appraisal of self. For at the heart of her philosophy is the understanding that **only we have the power to make ourselves happy and fulfilled** and our path to getting there is dependent on:

1. Being Honest With Ourselves

The only route to change and moving forward is to be **totally truthful** with yourself and what is going on in your life. While all of us engage in some form of self-denial, we eventually must make a very conscious choice to do something about our life. One thing for sure is we certainly don't have to be the victim of it, for the possibility of change can be wonderful and energizing if we orchestrate it. We have that power. While it may take some of us longer to decide to use it, once we do, we need to push up the volume and use it to our fullest advantage.

2. Being Our Own Best Advocate

While there are individuals in your life who care about you, love you, and want to do things to help you, at the end of the day you are and need to be your own best advocate. Let's face it, all of us, no matter how successful we are, struggle with our own demons, our own insecurities, and our own needs. The care and feeding of our own success must be a full-time job. Those who do it better are better able to help themselves and others. Be your own self-promoter. Be your own fan club. Most of all, **be your truest believer.**

3. Recognizing Life is a Pendulum

There is no question each of us is trying to achieve balance in our personal and professional lives. However, **before we can even come close to balance we need to recognize that life is a pendulum.** There will be ups and downs. There will be two steps forward and two steps backward. The way we cope with this reality impacts on our ability to achieve an emotional balance.

Even the language we use to describe how we feel affects how we see the world and how we address the world. Haven't each of us known individuals who are "catastrophisers," always choosing language and speaking in extremes, using words that suggest the worst case scenario rather than using language that is hopeful and inspires confidence? We have to engage in what is often referred to as the process of self-persuasion. The longer we say something, both publicly and privately to others, and to ourselves, the more we can counter the negative attitudes we may have held. We begin to take on a more positive view.

Visualize, Visualize, Visualize

At various times in this book, I have talked about giving yourself permission to chill out, do nothing, to maybe even think differently than you've ever thought before about your personal and your professional life. This freedom to dream, to be a bit "reckless" in your thoughts may be just what we all need to counter our complacency and our predictability.

Perhaps **a better word for dreaming is visualizing,** for if we have a clear picture of what we would like to be doing or where we would like to be, chances are greater that we will take the steps that are necessary to get there. Both professional athletes and inspirational and motivational speakers of all persuasions talk about the power of visualization in making personal and professional aspirations come true. Visualization takes work, and it takes perseverance but most of all, it takes optimism and a strong belief that we have the "goods" to get where we want to be, if only we take advantage of the opportunity.

Epilogue

By now you are no doubt curious as to how my own journey turned out, not that it will necessarily be the direction that you decide to take. After taking steps that you have read about in this book and weighing all the possibilities, I decided to start my own business. Wouldn't you know, in the midst of doing that I received an offer for a position that I simply could not refuse. How did it happen? Through reconnection, with individuals I hadn't seen in years but whose trust and confidence in me had not wavered.

I've continued with my exercise plan an have lost an additional ten pounds, and my wife still insists that my growth of new hair continues to accelerate as I keep changing. Regardless of whether or not this is true is irrelevant, since, after all , how you look at yourself and the belief you have in yourself are what ultimately matters. The truth is, there is no magic potion for change but just a matter of doing it. SO, Rogaine, step aside! My advice is just quit your job and grow some hair.

Career Resources

THE FOLLOWING CAREER RESOURCES ARE AVAILABLE directly from Impact Publications. Full descriptions of each title as well as nine downloadable catalogs, videos, and software can be found on our website: www.impactpublications.com. Complete the following form or list the titles, include shipping (see formula at the end), enclose payment, and send your order to:

IMPACT PUBLICATIONS
9104 Manassas Drive, Suite N
Manassas Park, VA 20111-5211 USA
1-800-361-1055 (orders only)
Tel. 703-361-7300 or Fax 703-335-9486
Email address: info@impactpublications.com
Quick & easy online ordering: www.impactpublications.com

Orders from individuals must be prepaid by check, money order, or major credit card. We accept telephone, fax, and email orders.

Qty.	TITLES	Price	TOTAL
Featured Title			
_____	Quit Your Job and Grow Some Hair	$15.95	_____
Changing Careers			
_____	Career Change	14.95	_____
_____	Change Your Job, Change Your Life (8th Edition)	17.95	_____
_____	Complete Idiot's Guide to Changing Careers	17.95	_____
_____	Is It Too Late to Run Away and Join the Circus?	16.95	_____
_____	Me, Myself, and I, Inc.	17.95	_____
_____	The Portable Executive	12.00	_____
_____	Rites of Passage at $100,000 to $1 Million+	29.95	_____
_____	Switching Careers	17.95	_____

Inspiration and Empowerment

_____	101 Secrets of Highly Effective Speakers	15.95 _____
_____	Do What You Love for the Rest of Your Life	24.95 _____
_____	Do What You Love, the Money Will Follow	13.95 _____
_____	Doing Work You Love	14.95 _____
_____	Eat That Frog!	19.95 _____
_____	Habit-Busting	13.00 _____
_____	Life Strategies	13.95 _____
_____	Maximum Success	24.95 _____
_____	Power of Purpose	20.00 _____
_____	Practical Dreamer's Handbook	13.95 _____
_____	Right Words at the Right Time	25.00 _____
_____	Self Matters	26.00 _____
_____	Seven Habits of Highly Effective People	14.00 _____
_____	Who Moved My Cheese?	19.95 _____

Attitude and Motivation

_____	100 Ways to Motivate Yourself	18.99 _____
_____	Change Your Attitude	15.99 _____
_____	Reinventing Yourself	18.99 _____

Testing and Assessment

_____	Career Interests to Job Chart	19.95 _____
_____	Career Tests	12.95 _____
_____	Discover the Best Jobs for You	15.95 _____
_____	Discover What You're Best At	14.00 _____
_____	Do What You Are	18.95 _____
_____	Finding Your Perfect Work	16.95 _____
_____	Gifts Differing	16.95 _____
_____	I Could Do Anything If Only I Knew What It Was	13.95 _____
_____	I'm Not Crazy, I'm Just Not You	16.95 _____
_____	Making Vocational Choices	29.95 _____
_____	Now, Discover Your Strengths	27.00 _____
_____	Pathfinder	15.00 _____
_____	Please Understand Me II	15.95 _____
_____	TalentSort: The Career Decision Card Sort	29.95 _____
_____	What Type Am I?	14.95 _____
_____	What's Your Type of Career?	17.95 _____

Career Exploration and Job Strategies

_____	25 Jobs That Have It All	12.95 _____
_____	50 Cutting Edge Jobs	15.95 _____
_____	95 Mistakes Job Seekers Make	13.95 _____
_____	100 Great Jobs and How to Get Them	17.95 _____
_____	101 Careers	16.95 _____

_____	101 Ways to Recession-Proof Your Career	14.95 _____
_____	Adams Jobs Almanac	16.95 _____
_____	Age Advantage	12.95 _____
_____	American Almanac of Jobs and Salaries	20.00 _____
_____	America's Top Jobs for People Without a Four-Year Degree	15.95 _____
_____	Back Door Guide to Short-Term Job Opportunities	21.95 _____
_____	Best Computer Jobs in America	18.95 _____
_____	Best Jobs for the 21st Century	19.95 _____
_____	Best Keywords for Resumes, Cover Letters, Interviews	17.95 _____
_____	Break the Rules	15.00 _____
_____	Career Guide to Environmental Careers	17.95 _____
_____	Career Guide to Industries	16.95 _____
_____	Career Intelligence	15.95 _____
_____	Careers in Criminology	16.95 _____
_____	Cool Careers for Dummies	19.99 _____
_____	Dancing Naked	17.95 _____
_____	Directory of Executive Recruiters	47.95 _____
_____	Directory of Holland Occupational Codes	54.00 _____
_____	Enhanced Guide for Occupational Exploration	34.95 _____
_____	Enhanced Occupational Outlook Handbook	37.95 _____
_____	Five Secrets to Finding a Job	12.95 _____
_____	Health-Care Careers for the 21st Century	24.95 _____
_____	Help! Was That a Career Limiting Move?	10.95 _____
_____	High-Tech Careers for Low-Tech People	14.95 _____
_____	How to Be a Permanent Temp	12.95 _____
_____	How to Be a Star at Work	12.00 _____
_____	How to Get a Job and Keep It	16.95 _____
_____	How to Succeed Without a Career Path	13.95 _____
_____	Insider's Guide to Finding the Perfect Job	14.95 _____
_____	Internships	26.95 _____
_____	Job Search Handbook for People With Disabilities	16.95 _____
_____	Job Smarts	16.95 _____
_____	JobBank Guide to Computer and High-Tech Jobs	17.95 _____
_____	Knock 'Em Dead	12.95 _____
_____	No One Is Unemployable	29.95 _____
_____	No One Will Hire Me!	13.95 _____
_____	Occupational Outlook Handbook	16.95 _____
_____	O*NET Dictionary of Occupational Titles	39.95 _____
_____	The Professional's Job Finder	18.95 _____
_____	Quit Your Job and Grow Some Hair	15.95 _____
_____	Sunshine Jobs	16.95 _____
_____	What Color Is Your Parachute?	17.95 _____

Internet Job Search

_____	100 Top Internet Job Sites	12.95 _____
_____	Adams Internet Job Search Almanac	10.95 _____
_____	America's Top Internet Job Sites	19.95 _____

_____ CareerXroads (annual)	26.95	_____
_____ Career Exploration On the Internet	24.95	_____
_____ Cyberspace Job Search Kit	18.95	_____
_____ Directory of Websites for International Jobs	19.95	_____
_____ e-Resumes	11.95	_____
_____ Electronic Resumes and Online Networking	13.99	_____
_____ Everything Online Job Search Book	12.95	_____
_____ Guide to Internet Job Searching	14.95	_____
_____ Haldane's Best Employment Websites for Professionals	15.95	_____
_____ Job-Hunting On the Internet	9.95	_____
_____ Job Search Online for Dummies (with CD-ROM)	24.99	_____

Resumes and Letters

_____ 101 Best .Com Resumes and Letters	11.95	_____
_____ 101 Best Cover Letters	11.95	_____
_____ 101 Best Resumes	10.95	_____
_____ 101 Great Resumes	9.99	_____
_____ 101 More Best Resumes	11.95	_____
_____ 101 Great Tips for a Dynamite Resume	13.95	_____
_____ 175 High-Impact Cover Letters	14.95	_____
_____ 175 High-Impact Resumes	14.95	_____
_____ 201 Dynamite Job Search Letters	19.95	_____
_____ 201 Killer Cover Letters	16.95	_____
_____ $100,000 Resumes	16.95	_____
_____ Adams Resume Almanac, with Disk	19.95	_____
_____ America's Top Resumes for America's Top Jobs	19.95	_____
_____ Asher's Bible of Executive Resumes	29.95	_____
_____ Best Cover Letters for $100,000+ Jobs	24.95	_____
_____ Best Resumes and CVs for International Jobs	24.95	_____
_____ Best Resumes for $100,000+ Jobs	24.95	_____
_____ Best Resumes for $75,000+ Executive Jobs	15.95	_____
_____ Big Red Book of Resumes	16.95	_____
_____ Building a Great Resume	15.00	_____
_____ Building Your Career Portfolio	13.99	_____
_____ Cover Letter Magic	16.95	_____
_____ Cover Letters for Dummies	16.99	_____
_____ Cover Letters That Knock 'Em Dead	10.95	_____
_____ Cyberspace Resume Kit	18.95	_____
_____ Dynamite Cover Letters	14.95	_____
_____ Dynamite Resumes	14.95	_____
_____ e-Resumes	11.95	_____
_____ Electronic Resumes and Online Networking	13.99	_____
_____ Everything Cover Letter Book	12.95	_____
_____ Everything Resume Book	12.95	_____
_____ Expert Resumes for Computer and Web Jobs	16.95	_____
_____ Federal Resume Guidebook	21.95	_____
_____ Gallery of Best Cover Letters	18.95	_____

_____ Gallery of Best Resumes	18.95	_____
_____ Global Resume and CV Guide	17.95	_____
_____ Haldane's Best Cover Letters for Professionals	15.95	_____
_____ Haldane's Best Resumes for Professionals	15.95	_____
_____ High Impact Resumes and Letters (8th Edition)	19.95	_____
_____ Insider's Guide to Writing the Perfect Resume	14.95	_____
_____ Internet Resumes	14.95	_____
_____ Military Resumes and Cover Letters	19.95	_____
_____ Overnight Resume	12.95	_____
_____ Power Resumes	12.95	_____
_____ Professional Resumes for Executives, Managers, & Other Administrators	19.95	_____
_____ Professional Resumes for Accounting, Tax, Finance, and Law	19.95	_____
_____ Proven Resumes	19.95	_____
_____ Resume Catalog	15.95	_____
_____ Resume Kit	14.95	_____
_____ Resume Magic	18.95	_____
_____ Resume Shortcuts	14.95	_____
_____ Resumes for Dummies	16.99	_____
_____ Resumes for the Health Care Professional	14.95	_____
_____ Resumes in Cyberspace	14.95	_____
_____ Resumes That Knock 'Em Dead	12.95	_____
_____ The Savvy Resume Writer	12.95	_____
_____ Sure-Hire Resumes	14.95	_____

Networking

_____ Connecting With Success	20.95	_____
_____ Dynamite Telesearch	12.95	_____
_____ A Foot in the Door	14.95	_____
_____ Golden Rule of Schmoozing	12.95	_____
_____ Great Connections	11.95	_____
_____ How to Work a Room	14.00	_____
_____ Make Your Contacts Count	14.95	_____
_____ Masters of Networking	16.95	_____
_____ Networking for Everyone	16.95	_____
_____ Networking Smart	22.95	_____
_____ Power Networking	14.95	_____
_____ Power Schmoozing	12.95	_____
_____ Power to Get In	14.95	_____
_____ The Savvy Networker	13.95	_____
_____ The Secrets of Savvy Networking	13.99	_____

Dress, Image, and Etiquette

_____ Dressing Smart for Men	14.95	_____
_____ Dressing Smart for Women	14.95	_____
_____ Dressing Smart for the New Millennium	15.95	_____

_____ First Five Minutes   14.95   _____
_____ New Professional Image   12.95   _____
_____ New Women's Dress for Success   13.99   _____
_____ Power Etiquette   15.95   _____
_____ Professional Impressions   14.95   _____

Interviews

_____ 101 Dynamite Answers to Interview Questions   12.95   _____
_____ 101 Dynamite Questions to Ask At Your
      Job Interview   13.95   _____
_____ 101 Great Answers to the Toughest
      Interview Questions   11.99   _____
_____ Behavior-Based Interviewing   12.95   _____
_____ Best Answers to the 201 Most Frequently Asked
      Questions   11.95   _____
_____ Great Interview   12.95   _____
_____ Haldane's Best Answers to Tough Interview Questions 15.95   _____
_____ Interview for Success (8th Edition)   15.95   _____
_____ Interview Power   14.95   _____
_____ Interview Rehearsal Book   12.00   _____
_____ Job Interviews for Dummies   16.99   _____
_____ Power Interviews   15.95   _____
_____ The Savvy Interviewer   10.95   _____
_____ Sweaty Palms   12.95   _____
_____ Winning Interviews for $100,000+ Jobs   17.95   _____

Salary Negotiations

_____ 101 Salary Secrets   12.95   _____
_____ Better Than Money   18.95   _____
_____ Dynamite Salary Negotiations   15.95   _____
_____ Get a Raise in 7 Days   14.95   _____
_____ Get More Money On Your Next Job   17.95   _____
_____ Get Paid More and Promoted Faster   19.95   _____
_____ Haldane's Best Salary Tips for Professionals   15.95   _____
_____ Negotiating Your Salary   12.95   _____

Government and Nonprofit Jobs

_____ Complete Guide to Public Employment   19.95   _____
_____ Directory of Federal Jobs and Employers   21.95   _____
_____ Education Job Finder   18.95   _____
_____ Federal Applications That Get Results   23.95   _____
_____ Federal Employment From A to Z   14.50   _____
_____ Federal Jobs in Law Enforcement   14.95   _____
_____ FBI Careers   18.95   _____
_____ Find a Federal Job Fast!   15.95   _____
_____ From Making a Profit to Making a Difference   16.95   _____

_____ Government Job Finder 18.95 _____
_____ Jobs and Careers With Nonprofit Organizations 17.95 _____
_____ Nonprofits Job Finder 18.95 _____
_____ Ten Steps to a Federal Job 39.95 _____

International and Travel Jobs

_____ Back Door Guide to Short-Term Job Adventures 21.95 _____
_____ Best Resumes and CVs for International Jobs 24.95 _____
_____ Careers in International Affairs 17.95 _____
_____ Careers in Travel, Tourism, and Hospitality 19.95 _____
_____ Career Opportunities in Travel and Tourism 18.95 _____
_____ Directory of Jobs and Careers Abroad 16.95 _____
_____ Directory of Websites for International Jobs 19.95 _____
_____ Flight Attendant Job Finder and Career Guide 16.95 _____
_____ Global Citizen 16.95 _____
_____ Global Resume and CV Guide 17.95 _____
_____ How to Get a Job in Europe 21.95 _____
_____ How to Get a Job With a Cruise Line 16.95 _____
_____ How to Live Your Dream of Volunteering Overseas 17.00 _____
_____ Inside Secrets to Finding a Career in Travel 14.95 _____
_____ International Jobs 18.00 _____
_____ International Job Finder 19.95 _____
_____ Jobs for Travel Lovers 17.95 _____
_____ Living, Studying, and Working in Italy 17.00 _____
_____ Overseas Summer Jobs 17.95 _____
_____ So, You Want to Join the Peace Corps 12.95 _____
_____ Study Abroad 29.95 _____
_____ Summer Study Abroad 15.95 _____
_____ Teaching English Abroad 15.95 _____
_____ Teaching English Overseas 19.95 _____
_____ Work Abroad 15.95 _____
_____ Working Abroad 14.95 _____
_____ Work Your Way Around the World 17.95 _____

College-to-Career Resources

_____ 101 Best Resumes for Grads 11.95 _____
_____ 200 Best Jobs for College Graduates 16.95 _____
_____ America's Top Jobs for College Graduates 15.95 _____
_____ Best Jobs for the 21st Century for College Graduates 19.95 _____
_____ Best Resumes for College Students and New Grads 12.95 _____
_____ College Grad Job Hunter 14.95 _____
_____ College Major Handbook 21.95 _____
_____ College Majors and Careers 16.95 _____
_____ College Majors Handbook 24.95 _____
_____ Complete Resume and Job Search Book for
College Students 12.95 _____
_____ Great Careers in Two Years 19.95 _____

_____ A Fork in the Road: A Career Planning Guide
for Young Adults   14.95   _____
_____ Gallery of Best Resumes for 2-Year Degree Graduates   18.95   _____
_____ Quick Guide to College Majors and Careers   16.95   _____
_____ Resumes for College Students and Recent Graduates   10.95   _____
_____ Ten Things I Wish I Knew Before Going Out
in the Real World   19.95   _____

Career Counselors

_____ Career Counselor's Handbook   17.95   _____
_____ Handbook of Career Counseling Theory   69.95   _____

Directories

_____ Almanac of American Employers   199.99   _____
_____ Almanac of American Employers Mid-Sized Firms   179.99   _____
_____ American Salaries and Wages Survey   175.00   _____
_____ Career Guide to Industries   16.95   _____
_____ Directory of Executive Recruiters   47.95   _____
_____ Directory of Holland Occupational Codes   54.00   _____
_____ Encyclopedia of Associations   575.00   _____
_____ Enhanced Guide for Occupational Exploration   34.95   _____
_____ Enhanced Occupational Outlook Handbook   37.95   _____
_____ Headquarters USA   175.00   _____
_____ Job Hunter's Sourcebook   115.00   _____
_____ National Job Bank   450.00   _____
_____ Occupational Outlook Handbook   16.95   _____
_____ O*NET Directory of Occupational Titles   39.95   _____
_____ Professional Careers Sourcebook   125.00   _____
_____ Scholarships, Fellowships, and Loans   199.00   _____
_____ Vocational Careers Sourcebook   115.00   _____
_____ Worldwide College Scholarship Directory   23.99   _____
_____ Worldwide Graduate Scholarship Directory   26.99   _____

Audiocassettes

_____ 101 Secrets of Highly Effective Speakers   16.95   _____
_____ Get a Raise in 7 Days   16.95   _____
_____ The Savvy Networker   16.95   _____

Videos

_____ Build a Network for Work and Life   149.00   _____
_____ Make a Good First Impression   129.00   _____
_____ Ten Commandments of Resumes   98.00   _____
_____ Think Small: Finding Big Jobs in Small Businesses   149.00   _____
_____ Tips and Techniques to Improve Your Total Image   98.00   _____
_____ Why Should I Hire You?   129.00   _____

Software

_____ 12 Biggest Mistakes Job Hunters and Career
Changers Make and How to Avoid Them   149.95   _____
_____ Job Browser Pro 1.3   359.95   _____

SUBTOTAL   _____

Virginia residents add 4½% sales tax   _____

POSTAGE/HANDLING ($5 for first
product and 8% of SUBTOTAL) $5.00

8% of SUBTOTAL --   _____

TOTAL ENCLOSED ------------------------   _____

SHIP TO:

NAME _____

ADDRESS _____

_____

_____

PAYMENT METHOD:

❑ I enclose check/money order for $ _____ made payable to
    IMPACT PUBLICATIONS.

❑ Please charge $ _____ to my credit card:
    ❑ Visa   ❑ MasterCard   ❑ American Express   ❑ Discover

    Card # _____ Expiration date: ____/____

    Signature _____